SECRETS OF MOUND GARDENING

HARNESSING NATURE FOR HEALTHIER FRUITS, VEGGIES, AND ENVIRONMENT

GREEN GARDEN
SYSTEMS

darryl@greengardensystems.com

ISBN: 978-1-7363136-0-2 (paperback)
ISBN: 978-1-7363136-2-6 (hardcover)
ISBN: 978-1-7363136-1-9 (ebook)

Ordering Information:
Special discounts are available on quantity purchases by corporations, associations, and others. For details, contact darryl@greengardensystems.com

SECRETS OF MOUND GARDENING

HARNESSING NATURE FOR HEALTHIER FRUITS, VEGGIES, AND ENVIRONMENT

DARRYL WHITHAM

DEDICATION

I dedicate this to our brethren throughout history—including the many gardeners today—who have contributed to our knowledge of ecologically friendly gardening. This knowledge, especially from ancient sources passed down in oral or written formats, must be saved and utilized, as it was developed out of necessity and contains many truths born out of millennia of observation. Embrace the mound and celebrate the harvest as the ancients once did.

AUTHOR'S NOTE

My goal with this book is to teach people how to feed themselves and help save the world at the same time. The days of living in contention with nature must come to an end. We must learn to nurture and work with nature instead of trying to conquer it. Natural processes and cycles have been in existence for billions of years, and the short destructive reign by humans has brought our ecological systems to their knees. If we are to survive, we must give honor and thanks to nature and embrace her ways. And if we don't, humans will be the ones who suffer the most.

TABLE OF CONTENTS

CHAPTER 1

WHAT IS A MOUND GARDEN?

"If you have a garden and a library, you have everything you need."
—Cicero, Roman statesman and citizen[1]

I **have always loved** plants. When I was a kid growing up in Connecticut, I would look forward to visiting my grandparents' house because I could work with them in their garden. They had a huge garden with all kinds of plants—a raised area for azalea bushes, horseradish growing in the back, and even gooseberries. It was at a young age working with those plants when I first fell in love with gardening. When my grandparents passed away, my mother purchased their house from her brothers, and I moved in to keep their garden going. Gardening became more than just a relaxing hobby; it became a passion that brought me a sense of joy and wonder that truly felt mystical.

After high school, I continued living at home with my parents while I attended Housatonic Community College. While going to school, I took a job at a greenhouse that hired a lot of local students. That greenhouse would receive shipments of exotic and carnivorous plants, and I would research what I could find about them. In our little office, we had a giant plant encyclopedia, about eight inches thick, that provided all the information one would ever need about these plants, and I must have read that book cover to cover multiple times.

I was hooked, but my obsession didn't end with research. It was my job to care for the plants and remove the dead leaves. If a plant was misshapen, I'd make cuttings, but instead of throwing those cuttings away, I would keep them in a wet paper towel and then take them home and root them. Pretty soon, I had covered my parents' deck with all types of rare plants—pitcher plants, Venus flytraps, and sundews. I knew how rare those plants were and that their habitat was being destroyed, so I wanted to reproduce them and maybe even sell them at plant shows.

That feeling has only increased with age. Now that I'm older and have settled down with my family in Virginia, I have become a certified square-foot gardener and a certified straw-bale gardener. I want to pass along what I have learned, so I teach a series of classes on hydroponics and square-foot gardening through my county's parks and recreation program and hope that I can teach more in the future.

I often wonder what's at the root of my obsession. Now that I no longer have an appetite for the dry tastelessness of the average industrial-grade tomato foisted upon us at the supermarket, maybe what drives me is the craving to taste the fresh, ripe goodness of a juicy homegrown tomato, picked right from my own garden. It might be the excitement I get from using ancient techniques to harvest my own heirloom crop. It could be the rush of creating something where there was once nothing. Perhaps there is some ancient recessive gene I inherited from my family's Carpathian Mountain past that gives me this inclination. It might be a combination of all of that, but recently I've realized that my love goes beyond the actual crops. It's the systems themselves that fascinate me. I love learning about ancient techniques and their history. That is what first drew me to mound gardening.

Gardening may be fun, but nobody ever said that it was easy. As much as I looked forward to working in my grandparents' garden as a kid, it was still a chore. With conventional gardening, you have to dig up a large plot and flip the whole area over with a shovel. You could rent a rototiller, but that's no picnic either. If the soil is too dry, it could turn to dust. If it's too wet, it could damage the soil. And if you have clay soil, you could wind up with big clumps of clay. You must also fertilize the entire area, using Miracle-Gro or other chemical fertilizers popular with home gardeners. Then you need to create rows and spaces between those rows, but weeds will surely pop up all over. So, you begin what becomes a continuous cycle of feeding and weeding because, once you turn over the soil, you're opening it up for weeds. Many novice gardeners get frustrated and quit when their efforts don't turn out as expected, but gardening doesn't have to be so difficult.

Mound gardening is different because, regardless of your level of experience, you can produce organic, healthy vegetables without the hours of tedious labor often associated with conventional gardening. A mound garden is just like it sounds—a series of small, easily managed garden plots. You don't have to waste your energy by digging up and tilling a large area. Fertilizer isn't required because you build the soil. Weeding is confined to a small area, and if you utilize mulch, you'll have even fewer weeds. In my estimation, with mound gardening, there is an 80 to 90 percent reduction in weeding, feeding, and overall work. It takes only a few minutes each day for you to help the environment while reaping the benefits of the delicious fruits and vegetables produced during your harvest.

Over the years, I have learned how to make gardening easy for busy people like me, and I want to pass on that knowledge. Despite my obsession, I do a whole lot more than gardening. I am a father and a foster parent. I work full-time in information technology and have grown used to 12-hour workdays. I am an advocate for the environment. I love hiking in the beautiful surroundings of where I live in Northern Virginia. If I can make time for gardening, anyone can! I currently live on two acres, with roughly one-eighth of an acre in use, and I have a lot of little plots and test beds that I can manage in the mornings before work.

The systems and techniques I share throughout these chapters have made gardening so easy for my family and some of the other forms of gardening I have utilized have even allowed me to grow corn and pumpkins on my deck.

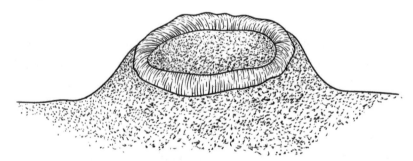

NATIVE AMERICAN MOUND WITH WATER HOLDING SOIL RIM

Mound gardening certainly isn't anything new—far from it. Planting crops in mounds has benefited man since the dawn of agriculture. Over the years, many types of mound-garden structures have been developed, each utilizing and adapting to the soil and resources available in that general region. For hundreds of years, various Native American tribes have utilized mound-gardening techniques, long before there were chemical fertilizers and rototillers. Native Americans planted in small soil mounds that benefited their crops.[2] The Aztecs utilized *chinampas*, which are long, narrow, raised garden mounds separated by water canals and composed of decaying vegetation, dirt, and mud.[3]

In this book, we'll dive into some of the history and lay out various gardening methods while focusing on six of the main types of mound gardens that you can easily create in your own backyard.

1. Survival mounds.

2. Native American mounds.

3. Hügelkultur mounds.

4. Keyhole mounds.

5. Raised-bed mounds.

6. Compost, or midden mounds.

I will share insights, stories, tricks, tips, and lessons that I've learned over the years from my personal experience with each of these types. I will be with you every step of the way when deconstructing the exact methods utilized by the ancients and by modern gardeners. These methods can be used by permaculturists, survival gardeners, those with only a small garden area, and anyone who loves interesting and effective gardening techniques. By the end of the book, you will know which mounds are best suited for your own needs and you will have all the tools at your disposal to immediately get your own gardens up and running.

After the Victory Gardens of World War II, modern supermarkets and industrial farming became the norm, and now most people buy their fruits and vegetables from the store.[4] Although there are fewer gardeners today than 70 years ago, many of them are passionate about sustainably growing their own food while improving our environment. There is always room for more. It's never too late to enjoy one of humankind's oldest hobbies.

I hope that you can embrace some of these methods of the past to supplement your food supply by growing most, or even all, of your own food. If the 2020 coronavirus pandemic has taught us anything, it's that we never know when our lives, and the lives of our families, may depend on our ability to grow and provide our own food. You can do humankind a great favor by protecting genetic diversity. Think of organic crops as your vitamin for the day—freshly grown organic produce is the best medicine for your body. And when you make the time, you will find, as I have, that gardening can be not only fun, but also a life- and world-changing activity that brings you, your family, and your community years of pleasure and fulfillment. So, let's get started!

You can use this book as a step-by-step manual or as an end-table reference for successful gardening methods that go back to antiquity, but you don't have to wait until you get to the end of the book to get started. Following are two quick mound-garden methods that will get you up and gardening as fast as possible while also exposing you to some of the techniques that will be used later in the book.

THE TWO-MINUTE MOUND GARDEN—SOIL BAG MOUND METHOD

This method will allow you to get your garden started within the shortest period of time. First make sure to find a nice sunny location to place the mound garden. When your garden is completed, you can apply a layer of mulch to help prevent weeds and reduce the loss of soil moisture.

Materials:

You'll need only two two-cubic-foot bags of potting soil or potting mix. Try to go for a quality organic brand. A better option would be one bag of compost and one bag of potting mix, but if you are limited in resources, you can get away with only one bag of compost or potting mix.

The Process:

1. Place the soil bags in their final location after loosening the soil where the bags will lay. Use a rebar rod, large screwdriver, or pitchfork to loosen the soil. Cut the bags as shown in the diagram. You can place paper towels over the cut areas to hold the soil in when flipping the bags into their final location. Try to limit the amount of soil that falls out of the bags.

2. Place one bag on top of the other. If using one bag of compost and one bag of potting mix, make sure the compost bag is on the bottom.

3. Plant your seedling or seeds.

4. Congratulate yourself on making one of the fastest gardens ever!

5. Remember to add compost to the top of the bag mound at the end of the season.

A NICE TOUCH

Place stone, brick, or log framing around your soil bag mound garden to enhance the look of your new garden.

THE FIVE-MINUTE INSTANT MOUND GARDEN—COMPOST MOUND METHOD

This second method also allows you to get your garden started quickly, with the added benefit of getting rid of yard or kitchen waste. You'll want to gather the materials ahead of time, but you can get away with just using rich compost as the only ingredient. If you want even better results, build this mound during the fall, and plant the following spring. Before you get started, find the sunniest location to install your garden so that it has a minimum of six to eight hours of direct sun. Try to make sure this area doesn't flood and isn't chronically wet.

Materials:

a. One two-cubic-foot bag of potting soil or mix. Try to use a quality organic brand.

b. One large five-gallon bucket of mixed organic material, such as shredded dry leaves, non-treated dry grass clippings, plant-based kitchen scraps (ideally, organic), coffee grounds, all-paper teabags, or non-flowering weeds. You can also use purchased or premade compost for the organic material core. This organic material can be of just one type (like non-treated straw) if you do not have many materials on hand.

c. Non-glossy newspaper, cardboard, or shredded leaves.

The Process:

1. Quickly cut the grass on the chosen mound area with scissors, garden shears, a weedwhacker, or a lawnmower. This step is not critical since the turf will eventually die.

2. Use a shovel, stick, or small rebar rod to loosen or puncture multiple holes into the soil at an 18- to 48-inch diameter. Try to go down about 12 inches. This will allow water and nutrients to percolate down into the base soil.

3. Lay down a thick layer of non-glossy newspaper (10 to 13 pages), cardboard, or a quarter-inch layer of shredded leaves; moisten with water.

4. Pour the organic material or compost onto the wet newspaper to about eight inches high with only a tiny bit of compaction of the material.

5. Cap off this organic material with about three inches of the quality soil, gently pat the soil firm without excessively compacting it,

and have the mound extend out to the diameter that you had loosened in step 2.

6. Plant your seeds or seedlings. Keep the soil consistently moist (but not saturated) at least until the seeds have germinated or your seedlings have become established. Choose low-demand crops at first.

7. Congratulate yourself. You are now a mound builder!

Still have your doubts? Take comfort in the knowledge that you are not alone, and you are not the first to embark on this journey. You have the wisdom of the ancients to inspire you along the way. Don't forget that the universe will reward your good work when you seek to improve your world.

CHAPTER 2

PYRAMIDS OF PRODUCE

"Life begins the day you start a garden."
—Chinese proverb[5]

O ne of the benefits of mound gardening is that you can grow any crop you would grow in a conventional garden in your various mound gardens. The size of the mound, condition of the soil, and how well the mound is built will determine what crops will do best. Technically, you'd be able to grow a tree in your Hügelkultur mound, and if you can do that, you can grow pretty much anything else.

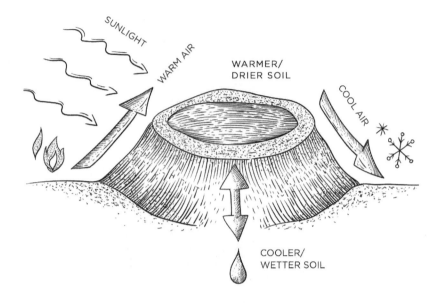

Not only is building your own mound garden simple and without limitation on the crops you can grow, it also allows you to greatly enhance the physical, biological, chemical, and environmental aspects of your garden location. The mound structure by itself induces temperature, moisture, humidity, and soil health changes to the immediate planting area. Essentially, a miniature mountain with subtle but different enough growth zones is created in such a small spot. There will be an altered microclimate on the top of the mound, which will manifest in temperature and moisture differences between the top and bottom of the feature. The mound will provide a mechanism to control plant density and spacing. The seedlings and plants will also be physically protected from soil tamping and soil crusting. But these aren't the only benefits. Consider also the following benefits.

This is your pyramid.

A mound garden stands out and adds dimension more than a conventional garden does. Just as the pyramids haven't been overlooked, you will be more inclined to enjoy the beauty of your mound garden while you care for your work of art.

These methods have lasted this long for a reason.

Mound gardening is a proven method that dates to antiquity. Throughout history, various Native American tribes and other cultures have depended on mound gardening for survival. Therefore, we know that they were built to be efficient and built to last.

Mound gardening provides climate adaptability.

Mound gardens can be designed to compensate for drought or excess rainfall, thus reducing the chances of the seeds rotting or withering. For example, you might need a reverse mound or a depression mound in arid regions. This isn't raised but is instead a depression or sunken area that captures rainfall like a sunken tub, so they work better than raised mounds in desert-like conditions where the raised mound would dry out. In drier climates, you'll need to pay more attention to watering mound gardens, since more soil surface area is exposed to the dryer air and the earth's insulating properties are negated. Mounds can be set up to rely only on rainfall for all their watering needs, whereas some other forms of gardening require drip lines, sprinklers, or hand watering.

You can garden more efficiently.

Mounds also allow the soil to warm up faster, due to more surface soil being impacted by sunlight, which speeds up germination. The raised mound will also extend the growing season by channeling the cooler air down and away from the mound.

There is no one right way to do it.

You have multiple options. Mound gardening is flexible in that it allows for many types of garden mound structures. You could build a mound garden that you won't have to water at all. Maybe you would like to honor Native American tribes of the past with an ancient-style mound garden. We'll lay out plenty of options in this book, so pick the one that is best for you.

You can decrease your carbon footprint.

How would you like a mound that disposes of and utilizes all of your kitchen waste? By building your mounds on top of pits full of your yard waste and kitchen scraps, you effectively get rid of this waste without the hassles of normal composting. We'll go into more details about these methods when discussing the Hügelkultur mounds. Compare this to composting that is done in an aboveground compost bin, which often doesn't look that great and has been known to attract insects and other pests. Mound gardening can be a great alternative.

It's fast and easy.

You can get started and build a mound garden in literally two minutes, as you've already discovered if you attempted to create either of the two examples explained in the previous chapter. Since the soil is already loose and friable, it's ready to utilize for current and subsequent plantings. It's also easier than furrow planting.

It's free or almost free.

Mound gardening can be free. Even if you choose to purchase soil materials for more predictable soil quality, which can possibly ensure better results, it will cost you very little money.

It may prevent the need for chemicals.

Forget about synthetic pesticides and herbicides. The intensive gardening characteristics of a polyculture mound will naturally crowd out weeds and confuse plant predators.

You don't need a lot of space.

Building a few polyculture mounds allows you to keep your garden small while having multiple crops that grow vertically at the same time. As you will read throughout this book, starting with a small garden is very wise, as gardening maintenance will be extremely negligible.

You can help combat climate uncertainty.

Recent climate change data indicates many more high precipitation events are to occur, the effects of which can be mitigated by planting on mounds.[6] In these days of economic and climate uncertainty, every family needs to have a backup food plan. As we saw during the pandemic in March 2020, grocery store shelves across the country were empty. That was bad, but it could always be so much worse. Now is the time to practice and become a more proficient gardener—and possibly become your neighborhood's first survival gardener, or permaculturist.

THE NATIVE AMERICAN WAY

The mound gardens of ancient Native Americans utilized many well-known modern permaculture methods such as polyculture, organic soil fertilization, raised grow areas, and basic composting. The Native Americans living in northern areas learned these methods out of necessity, as they depended on their harvest to get them through the winter. It is true that necessity is the mother of invention.

Source: Michael J. Caduto and Joseph Bruchac, *Native American Gardening: Stories, Projects, and Recipes for Families* (Golden, CO: Fulcrum Publishing, 1996): 71–72.

CHAPTER 3

THE MAGIC AND SCIENCE OF HEALTHY SOIL

"We don't inherit the earth from our ancestors;
we borrow it from our children."
—Wendell Berry, environmentalist.[7]

I t doesn't take much to form a mound. You can just dump a large
pile of nutrient-rich soil on the ground. It sounds simple, but what
happens is complex. The soil underneath will slowly improve over
time as the earthworms and biology of the soil transform the entire
mound, above and below. Soil is teeming with life, and what you add
to it will significantly affect that life. You can be a steward of the soil by
utilizing earth-friendly materials, which will also improve your chances
of a successful and bountiful garden.

Once built, the garden mounds follow permaculture rules of no plowing or tilling—only the surface area of the mound is loosened. This no-till method greatly reduces the oxidation and destruction of key soil nutrients while protecting the soil structure and soil organisms. Crops will thrive in the rich, healthy soil. Soil microbes and organisms also thrive in mound soil, because their habitats and specific soil zones are not disturbed as they are in tilled gardens. Healthy soil should translate into healthy crop growth.

The mound structure can also protect the crop seedlings. Seeds planted on the sides of the mound are more protected from hard pounding rains. The limited soil disturbance of mound gardening also prevents the mass weed invasion typical with large scale tilling. Mound gardening provides less risk of soil compaction from foot traffic because the mounds are clearly designated and visible. Also, you will not need to walk or tamp on the mounds, due to their size and spacing.

Consider the additional ways mound gardening can benefit the soil:

→ *Soil composition:* Mound gardening concentrates nutrients into single areas, not the areas between the mounds. It also maintains the soil's organic matter levels.

→ *Soil erosion:* The only soil that will be disturbed and exposed to the elements will be the mounds themselves, which constitute a much smaller part of the entire garden space. This initial erosion can be minimized with mulch, and when the crops get big enough, you can protect the mound soil surface with a plant canopy.

→ *Soil fertilization:* Mound gardening is an easy way to improve the soil's nutrient content and composition, as plant residues or compost is only added to the mound areas.

WHAT MAKES UP SOIL?

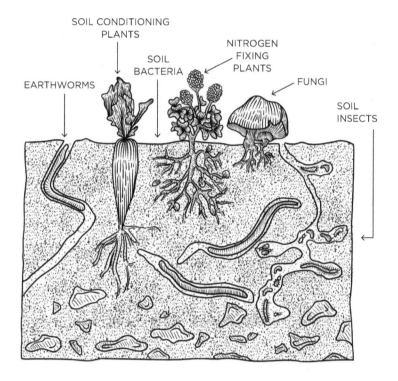

You'll know healthy soil when you see it, feel it, and smell it. It flows between your fingers. It's easy to work and crumble, and you can almost cup it in your hand. It will have a healthy, earthy smell that isn't swampy, rancid, or sour, which can happen if your soil is loaded with anaerobic activity and its byproducts. If there is plenty of oxygen available, even manure will decompose and develop into healthy soil, but if it remains wet and void of oxygen it will never become healthy. (That is what happens in swamps and sewers.)

The mounds that you build will be composed of soil in one form or another. The inorganic, or mineral, portion of soil is a mixture of three core materials: sand, silt, and clay. The amount of each of these three components in a soil determines the properties of it, as shown in the following examples:

→ Sandy soils drain much faster and hold fewer nutrients than healthy soil, due to the larger grain composition of the sand.[8] Cactuses might benefit from sandy soils, but food crops prefer a more nutrient-rich and water-retentive healthy soil.

→ Clay soils hold too much water and not enough air due to the extremely small particles that make up clay. Clay soils also become very hard when dry.[9] Food crops will struggle in a high clay soil environment due to the lack of air in the soil and the high retention of water in the minuscule spaces between the clay particles.

→ Healthy soil has the right amount of clay, sand, and silt, while also having plenty of organic materials and decayed living materials.[10]

💡 EXPERT TIP

Sandy and clay soils can be greatly improved by adding compost and other organic materials.

MY OWN EXPERIMENT

When I first moved to Northern Virginia in 2001, I learned that the soil in my area was a clay soil. From all of my research, I knew that clay soil was supposed to limit crop growth. But I wanted to see for myself, so I planted a series of crops in the clay soil just to see how they would perform. The lower-demand crops, such as kale or chard, didn't mind as much but crops like tomatoes and peppers did not thrive. Tomatoes and peppers require higher amounts of nutrients and sunlight; they have less of a temperature range for optimum growth, which makes these two crops require higher demands. In my experiment, I got fewer tomatoes, and the plants quickly withered away.

I didn't stop there. I tried all different combinations of fertilizers, products, and compost, and I came to one overwhelming conclusion—the variable that had the most positive impact by far was the health of the soil.

TESTING THE SOIL

If the quality of your soil is ever in doubt, test the soil before building your mound garden. Even if you feel that your soil is healthy, you should still test your soil every three years. You can perform a soil test with home test kits sold at garden centers, or you can send out a soil sample to a lab. You can also do your own simple soil tests.

Here are some simple home soil tests to use on existing yard soil:

Ribbon/Ball Test

You can form a ribbon or ball of soil with your hand to determine its composition. Pick up a small handful of moist soil and attempt to roll it into a ball. If it does not stick together and instead falls apart, then the soil is probably a sandy type of soil. If it forms a ball but still has a gritty sand-like feel, then it is probably a loamy type of soil. If it is very tacky, sticky, and has a shine when the ball is formed, then the soil sample is predominantly clay. The goal is to have a loamy type of soil.

Jar Test

Fill a one-quart mason jar halfway with the yard soil being tested. Add some clear water to fill the jar so that it's three-quarters full. Add a teaspoon of liquid dish soap. Secure the lid on the jar and shake the mixture for about four minutes. Let it rest for 24 hours and then observe the depth layer of sand, silt, and clay. Sand will be the bottom layer, followed by silt in the middle, and the top layer will be clay. The desired loamy-type soil will come in at 40 percent sand, 40 percent silt, and 20 percent clay.

Percolation Test

If you have purchased soil mix or made your own, you won't need to do this test because the soil should have the properties to drain sufficiently. If you haven't, start by digging a 12-by-12-inch hole and fill it to the top with water. When the water in the hole totally drains away, refill the hole to the top and monitor water drainage. Optimal drainage at this point will be a drop in the water level of one to two inches per hour. You can lay a straight stick across the hole to use as a level line to measure how many inches the water has dropped.

Compaction Test

Take a wire flag and plunge it vertically into the soil where the crops will be planted. If the wire flag can easily go down a foot or more without bending, then the soil is not showing signs of compaction. Compaction is not desired in garden soil, as it causes a reduced rate of both water infiltration and drainage. Another byproduct of compacted soil is reduced levels of critical soil gases such as oxygen, which often leads to poor plant growth and root rot. Root growth would also be negatively affected.

As you perform your soil tests, consider these soil-testing tips from the ancients:

Greek and Roman:[11]

→ Good soil should smell earthy and not swampy or foul when wet.

→ During a drought, the soil should not crack excessively, and during heavy rainfall, the water should not sit in puddles for a long duration. The water should soak into the soil rather quickly.

→ Good soil should be crumbly and very dark when moist and able to be easily squeezed into a loose ball.

→ During a frost, the soil should not form an ice shell on its surface.

→ Good soil will come from areas with large trees and not from areas that are full of small prickly shrubs.

Native American:[12]

→ Good soil will come from wooded areas along river floodplains.

→ Good soil will be easy to work and very dark to black in color.

→ Soil that is very dry and hard is not good soil to work with or to grow crops in.

→ Burn your garden brush on new garden areas to soften the soil.

→ Let the land lie fallow after the third year of gardening in a specific location. This will allow the soil to rejuvenate.

MIXTURES AND MINERALS

Don't underestimate the power of preparation. You'll want to enrich your soil before you plant. Ideally, this should be done in the fall or winter, which will give your soil a few months to settle in with the changes.

If you've tested your soil and know that it's poor, contaminated, or possibly diseased, you should use purchased soil mixes. This way you know that your mounds will contain quality soil without weeds, seeds, or diseased organisms. A purchased mix can ensure success, will give you a standard to go by, and should prevent any soil issues because of its pre-added nutrients, correct pH, and lack of disease organisms.

Improving the quality of your soil does not require a major purchase. You might only need basic items like topsoil and compost to build a healthy mound. Here is a simple method for instantly building your local soil:

1. Loosen the soil down about 12 inches deep.

2. Layer about three inches of nutrient-rich compost on top.

3. Gently turn the compost under. Plant a cover crop to keep this soil healthy for later use or build a mound on top using known nutrient rich soil.

4. Add an inch or two of mulch on top of the mound.

Your major goal is to have soil that is of the loamy type, which drains neither too fast nor too slowly. It should have the right amounts of sand, silt, clay, and organic matter. The soil you use for your mounds can be a mixture of some of the materials listed below. Any of these mixes can be used in any type of mound.

One of the benefits of mound gardening is that you don't have to use your own soil, so you can still garden even if your soil is contaminated—something you can't easily do with conventional gardening because you have so much more ground to cover. This way, your roots won't have to reach that contaminated soil. With mound gardening, you can buy or build your soil using any combination of the following materials.

Compost

Compost is a principal source of nutrients for your crops and probably one of the best. It contains a mixture of decomposed animal and plant waste materials. The best compost has multiple types of organic materials, such as mushrooms, manure, and leaf mold. You will find that your crops and soil will be better fertilized by a multisource compost, so if possible, try not to use a compost consisting of just one type of material, such as manure. Good compost can be purchased from a reputable source, but making your own compost is great way to reduce landfill waste and to feed and build your soil. Look for the other features of compost in the following chapter.

Soilless Mix

A soilless mix includes peat moss or coconut coir, vermiculite, and a blend of compost. If you're making the soilless mix yourself, you'll want to include equal volumes of each. You can find a more detailed description of these ingredients in the next section.

Soil Mix

A soil mix includes topsoil, sand, and a compost blend. If you're making the soil mix yourself, you'll want to include equal volumes of each. Pre-blended soil mixes that are ready to use can be purchased in either an organic or nonorganic formulation.

MATERIALS TO MAKE SOIL MIXES YOURSELF

The materials listed below are the various available components that allow you to make mound soil mixes yourself, as well as a brief explanation of specific materials and their benefits.

Pre-Compost Materials

Materials such as untreated dried lawn clippings, untreated straw, shredded leaves, vegetable kitchen scraps, dried nonflowering weeds, dried small twigs, and branches can be used in compost mounds or thrown into your compost pits or midden mounds.

Topsoil

Topsoil is exactly what it sounds like—the top two to eight inches of the soil. The topsoil has the highest concentration of minerals and organisms, so it's also where the most activity occurs. Your goal is to build healthy topsoil in your garden areas instead of digging or purchasing it.

Vermiculite

Vermiculite is a silicate mineral (mica) that undergoes significant expansion when heated. The heating creates numerous microcavities that hold lots of water and air, which are ideal ingredients for healthy plant growth. This is usually added at the time the soil mix is made.

Perlite

Perlite is volcanic rock that is heated until it expands into a light, airy, pebble-sized material. The numerous nooks and crannies hold plenty of air and water while loosening soil to allow for better water drainage. One downside is that perlite is super lightweight, thus causing it to float to the soil surface when water is applied too fast. This is also typically added at the time the soil mix is made.

Sand

Sand is a naturally occurring granular material composed of finely divided rock and mineral particles (typically quartz). Sand has excellent drainage properties that lend well when mixed into heavy clay soils.

Peat Moss

Peat moss is a brown, powdery material derived from partially decayed vegetation or organic matter that is unique to natural areas called peat bogs. Peat moss holds lots of water and loosens soil due to its light airy properties. Since peat moss is not a quick renewable resource, some alternatives are available, such as coconut coir or PittMoss.

Soil Amendments

The three main nutrients for healthy soil are nitrogen, phosphorus, and potassium. You can purchase nutrient amendments to help you improve the health of your soil. These can be added when the mound is initially constructed, or they can be added before the next planting of a mound to replace the nutrients removed by the earlier crops.

Some crops, such as corn and tomatoes, are heavy feeders and would demand more nutrients. Crops such as peas and beans don't require as much, because they utilize nitrogen-fixing bacteria that pull nitrogen from the air and store it in the root nodules. If you're unsure, a good rule of thumb is that any crop with a big, fruiting body will be a heavier feeder, because they need more calcium to form the wall of the cells than do leafy crops (kale, lettuce, etc.), which are lower demand.

You don't need soil amendments if your soil is rich and nutrient dense, but I still recommend them because they can enhance crop growth and ensure proper plant nutrition. Soil amendments can be especially beneficial when trying to grow those crops that are ravenous, heavy feeders. They are also beneficial if you haven't been adding compost or utilizing a cover crop, or if your soil testing shows a deficiency. This is one reason why it's recommended that you start with low demand crops—it will be easier for you to get a harvest without having to worry about adding amendments.

Commercial chemical fertilizers will easily kill your crops if you use too much, but it's not the same with organic soil amendments. Though possible, it is unlikely to overdose your crops using organic amendments. Because it takes so long to break down, it is difficult to use too much organic material. Just follow the directions on how to use the various soil amendments, and you shouldn't have any problems.

Common soil amendments include the following ingredients:

→ *Rock dust:* Provides minerals and nutrients such as calcium, iron, magnesium, phosphorus, and potassium in addition to trace elements and micronutrients.

→ *Blood meal:* A good source of nitrogen.

→ *Bone meal:* A good source of phosphorus and calcium.

→ *Greensand:* Adds nutrients such as potash, iron, magnesium, silica, and other trace materials.

→ *Gypsum:* Good for loosening clay soils and adding nutrients such as calcium and sulfur.

Cover Crops

Not all of your crops are planted with the intention of harvesting them. Cover crops are crops planted typically to prevent soil erosion, but they also help to manage water, weeds, and pests while contributing to the overall health of the soil. All of the soil formulations above will require either amendments of compost or a cover crop each growing season.

Some popular cover crops are buckwheat, crimson clover, winter rye, and hairy vetch.

I prefer to use clover, which has different types that you can utilize. Constant soil building with organic amendments, compost, and the use of cover crops will ensure a healthy soil biome and healthy nutritious crops. In the next chapter, we will cover composting. Composting utilizes Mother Nature's special process of decomposition to make free plant nutrients and soil conditioners.

CHAPTER 4

HOW DO YOU COMPOST?

"If there were not plants, we would not be here. We breathe what they breathe out. This is how we learn from them."
—Keetoowah Cherokee teacher

The idea of composting makes some people think of buying those bulky compost bins and turning compost. Fortunately, those days are over—that is, if you can get past the garden shop sales page. I started with a compost tower, but quickly gave up on turning it. Getting rid of that tower proved to be a beneficial and rewarding experience. It also made things so much easier, because composting in a bin can get technical because the compost pile has to be just the right height and reach the right temperature. If the bin is too small or narrow, for example, the compost pile might not get hot enough to kill disease organisms or weed seeds and may cause a very slow decomposition process.

Many things can therefore go wrong when composting aboveground in a bin.

Creating your own compost is not only a natural method that can save you money, but it can help combat global warming by reducing carbon dioxide and other greenhouse gasses.[13] Composting is a gift from Mother Nature, so accept the sacred gift and utilize the easy ways to do it. This chapter offers some tips and tricks that can enrich your crops so that you can learn how to compost as nature does—in the ground or on top like a fresh layer of fall leaves—using two popular methods:

→ Compost pile

→ Pit composting

We'll explore these methods in detail in the following sections.

COMPOSTING METHODS

As I've said, composting in the ground offers advantages that using a compost bin doesn't. Another advantage is that worms have easier access to an inground compost pile, and worms provide an important benefit to composting. When creating compost in the ground, worms will eat and make tunnels that allow the water and oxygen to get in. They basically aerate the soil simply by digging down deeper. Even the worm waste is nutrient rich and loaded with bacteria, because worm castings are a collection of all the essential nutrients and bacteria created by worms. Worms are crucial to composting and creating worm castings, so instead of buying another product to add to your mound garden, you can let this occur naturally when creating your compost inground or aboveground.

MARCUS CATO (CATO THE ELDER) 234–149 BC

In *De Agri Cultura*, Marcus Cato explains that quality compost can be made without having livestock for manure: "I appreciate that there are certain kinds of farms on which it is impossible to keep either live stock or birds, yet even in such places it is a lazy farmer who lacks manure for he can collect leaves, rubbish from the hedge rows, and droppings from the highways without giving offense, and indeed earning gratitude, he can cut ferns from his neighbor's land and all these things he can mingle with the sweepings of the courtyard; he can dig a pit, like that we have counselled for the protection of stable manure, and there mix together ashes, sewage, and straw, and indeed every waste thing which is swept up on the place. But it is wise to bury a piece of oak wood in the midst of the compost, for that will prevent venomous snakes from lurking in it. This will suffice for a farm without the livestock."

Source: Marcus Porcius Cato and Harrison Fairfax, trans., *Cato's farm management: ecologues from the De re rustica of M. Porcius Cato* (Chicago: R.R. Donnelley, 1910).

Compost Pile

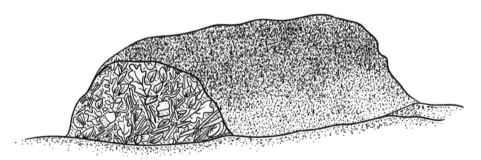

The compost pile method can be compared to sheet composting, which layers different compost materials similarly to how you'd make lasagna. As the name indicates, compost piles have, at their core, compostable material such as straw, leaves, or yard wastes. You can first lay down wet cardboard to suppress the weeds, then layer with three to six inches of leaves. Then add a layer of dried green grass followed by layers of yard waste, kitchen scraps, farm animal bedding, and farm animal waste. These materials can be piled up (not mixed together) so that they decompose over time. As we will discuss later in the chapter on midden mounds, this compost pile can become the site of a future mound garden.

Pit Composting

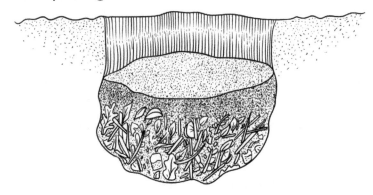

Pit composting (aka trench composting) is, as it sounds, when you dig a pit and throw your pre-compostable wastes into it. You then sit back and wait for Mother Nature to do her magic. This method of composting underground keeps the compost pile hidden.

Pit composting emulates the procedure of burying fish under a new mound, as Native Americans are believed to have done.[14] If you don't want to actually bury fish, you can use an organic fish fertilizer, which will provide all of the critical micronutrients that are so plentiful in ocean-caught fish. The Romans utilized deep pits to compost animal and human manure. They would also throw in animal bedding, food scraps, and bread-making waste.[15]

COMPOSTING PROCESS AND MATERIALS

If you want to try composting, you can use this tried-and-true method:

1. Dig a hole one-foot to three-feet deep, depending on the amount of compostable material that you have. The diameter of the hole can be determined by the size of the mound that you will build on top. These new compost pits can be placed between existing garden mounds, thus prepping your future grow areas.

2. Reduce the size of your compost materials. For best results, the source material should be chopped into very small pieces (smaller than two inches). Decomposition will occur much faster due to the increased surface area of the finely chopped waste material. A food processor, kitchen knife, or lawn mower can be used to reduce the size of the compostable materials. Another nifty way is to throw your materials into a garbage can and use a weed whacker to chop the material up.

3. Add the compostable material to the pit. Pour the well-mixed, finely chopped food scraps and yard waste into the hole in four-inch layers, then cover each four-inch layer with about one inch of soil or starter compost. Make sure each layer is moist. Place a board over the pit and weigh it down with rocks to prevent any critters from getting into the freshly brewed compost.

4. When the compost pit is full, cover it with nutrient-rich, healthy soil and then water it well. You will then be ready to create your mounds right on top of all the compost pit areas during the next growing season.

As you begin composting, consider using any of these common compostable materials:

→ Fresh, uncooked vegetable and fruit scraps (preferably organic).

→ Tea bags and coffee grounds (preferably organic).

→ Dried leaves (preferably shredded).

→ Untreated grass clippings.

→ Non-diseased plant materials not in seed.

→ Egg shells.

→ Pine needles.

→ Wood ash from untreated wood (limit the amount of wood ash, as it can change soil pH).

→ Straw (non-herbicide treated).

→ Cow, horse, chicken, or rabbit manure (ideally, animals that have not been fed with herbicide-treated materials).

→ Limited amounts of small-particle wood materials (avoid thick wood, branch materials, and any treated lumber).

→ Human urine.

If you still need convincing, consider these additional benefits of composting:

→ With pit composting, the composting process works year-round, due to the insulating properties of the ground and the heat generated by the composting process. You will also get completed compost much faster.

→ It will act as a water-holding area if the pits are close to your active growing mounds.

→ Both methods allow you to grow crops on your compost pile as the process progresses.

→ There is no need to purchase composting equipment, such as compost cages, towers, or tumblers, which require you to turn the compost.

→ It's an efficient way to rid your yard of leaves and grass clippings. Your kitchen scraps, tea bags, and coffee grounds are fair game, too! Just make sure your grass clippings are not from a chemically treated lawn. Kitchen scraps should ideally be organic, but don't let this hold you back if you're not an organic fanatic.

→ If you make enough compost, you will no longer need to buy commercial fertilizers.

→ It reduces the amount of waste that you send to the landfill.

→ Compost is a soil conditioner that balances the pH and improves structure.

→ It can function as a free mulch with the extra benefit of controlling soil erosion.

→ Its use may help to reduce pests and the chance of disease.

→ It helps to retain soil moisture, which means less watering is required.

→ Compost will attract and support beneficial fungi, bacteria, and larger soil life such as worms.

ADDITIONAL COMPOSTING CONSIDERATIONS

Earlier in this chapter, you learned which materials work best for composting, but not all materials are ideal for composting. I recommend that you not add animal products such as bones, fats, meats, grease, or dairy items to your compost pile, as they can attract rodents or breed harmful microorganisms. Dung from meat-eating animals, such as cats and dogs, should not be used in your compost pit, as it can also harbor harmful organisms. Also, do not throw diseased crop residues into your compost pile. However, in a survival situation, many rules go out the window. You can pretty much throw any material that was living into the compost with very few exceptions.

Here are some additional composting ideas that can be utilized if you want to do something different than or in addition to the pit composting or composting pile methods.

Chop and Drop Composting

More related to mulching, chop and drop is the practice of growing certain plants that will be grown, chopped, and then dropped on the garden's surface to perform immediate mulching functions, and, eventually, a composting function. Certain plants such as comfrey, red clover, and pigeon peas are nutrient dense and provide many macronutrients and micronutrients when they decompose in place. Another quick trick is to collect your coffee grounds and tea bags daily and spread them on top of your mounds as an even faster method of chop and drop. Maybe it would be more appropriate to call this method "drink and drop."

Leaf Mold Compost

It is simple to create leaf mold compost with black plastic lawn bags or meshed leaf bags. Just bag your leaves, or whatever materials you may have an excess of, and store them under a tree for at least six months to a year. That's it!

Making Compost Tea

Throughout the millennia, humankind grew very large and successful gardens by using natural methods. If you want to follow in their footsteps, try making your own compost tea. Compost teas are liquid solutions made from steeping compost in water for several days. Ideally, these teas should be made from the compost gathered from the bottom of your richest compost piles, specifically the piles that have a vast array of pre-compostable materials. This will help ensure that your compost tea will be as nutrient dense as possible.

Compost teas can be complicated or easy to make, depending on the desired microbe strength of the tea. The most microbially active teas require aquarium air pumps and air stones to provide the high aerobic aeration that will greatly boost the tea's microbe life. You can make compost tea by following the same steps as the ancients:

1. Fill a bucket one-third full of quality compost.

2. Add chlorine-free, quality water until just below the top of the bucket.

3. Let it sit for one to two days. Stir occasionally.

4. Strain the compost tea and dilute this concentrate with clear, fresh water when applying to your crops.

The steeping action extracts nutrients and microbes, which make a nutritious plant food and an effective soil microbe inoculation of the receiving soil. This tea can then be poured right into the soil. These teas can also be sprayed onto to the leaves to not only feed the plants, but also prevent leaf diseases. This will act as a fertilizer, because all leaves, unless they are super waxy, can absorb nutrients through the leaves. The compost tea can protect the plants from bacterial infections.

If you choose to spray it on the leaves, you will want a more filtered variety of the tea. Due to the high microbe load in the teas, be careful about eating aboveground plant materials if they have been provided by a foliar feeding with a compost tea. Plants growing in poorer soil can also get a nutrient boost with an application of compost tea.

CONCLUDING THOUGHTS ON COMPOSTING

When determining which composting methods to use, it comes down to what pre-compost materials you have available and how much time and labor you want to put into the process. For example, if you have excess tree leaves, you might want to bag them up and let Mother Nature turn them into leaf mold. Keep in mind that the methods that utilize the biggest collection of diverse materials in the same pit will be the most nutrient dense. Being able to utilize these methods will make you a composting grandmaster, but when all else fails, you can purchase compost.

If you need to purchase your initial compost supply, you can follow these steps to ensure that you are getting microbe-rich, quality compost:

1. Buy locally made and organic compost if possible. Ideally, you want to purchase a blended organic compost.

2. Look for a dark brown to almost black color.

3. The compost should smell earthy, not swampy, sour, or ammonia-like.

4. The compost should consist of mostly small particles, not large chunks, twigs, or sticks.

5. The compost should be slightly moist, but not soaking wet.

In the next chapter, you'll learn the details for how to plan your mound garden. A little bit of planning will help you build a healthy and productive garden.

CHAPTER 5

LOCATION, LOCATION, LOCATION

"To forget how to dig the earth and to tend the soil is to forget ourselves."
—M. Gandhi[16]

I've always been fascinated by Byzantine history and the Roman Empire. It might be because my family is from Eastern Europe. My mother is second generation and I'm third.

A major part of the history that appealed to me was gardening, particularly a book called *Geoponika*, which is a massive 20-book collection of ancient Greek and Roman gardening techniques compiled in Constantinople during the 10th century for the emperor Constantine VII.[17] One name that is peppered throughout this collection is a popular writer and horticulturist of third century Rome named Florentinus. Since modern-day gardening derived from these ancient Greek and Roman sources, I've created a plaque that hangs in my home and lists the following rules of gardening that Florentinus laid out almost 2,000 years ago. This is a reminder to myself, and it's something I rely on to help keep the spirit of that ancient culture alive.

Florentinus' Rules of Gardening include the following:

1. Gardening is essential to life.

2. The garden must be kept close to the house for the benefit to the mind and body and for the health of the garden.

3. Make your garden a pleasure to your senses of sight and smell (include aromatic plants as companion plants, for example).

4. Use quality seeds, suitable soil, a good water source, and quality manure.

5. Make sure you harvest continuously and only in the morning when the garden is covered in dew.

6. Make sure you choose your garden location wisely; interplant and use cuttings from your hardiest plants. (Interplant with flowers to attract bees and other beneficial insects.)

7. Keep a journal.

8. The garden overseer (you) must set an example to other gardeners.

No two gardens are the same. Everyone starts in a different place and attempts to build their garden under different conditions. Some people have more land to work with than others. The list can go on and on, but there are some basic criteria to consider when planning out your mound garden.

Garden Size

The size of the garden you start with can have a profound impact on your initial impressions of gardening. Let's say you invest a lot of time and money into creating a massive garden only for a powdery mildew plague to take hold. To save your crops, you would have to start by spraying every leaf with a fungal spray (hopefully environmentally safe). You'd have to keep reapplying to the point where this could become overwhelming for a novice gardener and leave a bad taste in their mouth.

If you had started with a smaller mound garden, the results would be different. With a smaller garden, you would likely have paid more attention to the whole garden and not missed the middle plants that first became afflicted with the disease. You also would have spent considerably less time spraying your plants, and your applications would probably have been more thorough.

The lesson here is don't overplant or start too large a garden. This may sound obvious, but it's our natural instinct to try and plant as much as possible. People try to overdo it to get more out of less area, and that immediately creates a water problem, which is why gardening books warn against this.

Starting small will not only make your garden experience more fruitful, but it will instill an urge for a larger garden in subsequent growing seasons. The Native Americans were known for starting small and slowly adding to their gardens over the next few seasons.[18,19] The ancillary benefit is that you gain more experience, so you can learn how local climate affects your crops while also observing some of the signs in nature that can guide your planting dates, such as when crops grow best, when pests hatch, and when to expect insect invasions.

Mound Garden Location

Equally as important as size is choosing the location of your mound garden. We've gone over different ways you can improve the poor soil at a growing location, but even the best soil might not be enough if you choose a poor growing location. That's why you want to take the time to scout out the best possible location for your mound garden first.

Another reason why starting small is a good idea is that you can scatter a few mounds in different locations to see which ones perform best, and then build your larger garden in the successful locations. Hopefully, your best location is by your house. (Remember Florentinus' rules?) Not only will this help you protect your crops, but it also comes with the benefit of being able to see your garden every time you leave and return to your house. The benefits of visiting your mound garden often cannot be overstated.

One area in which to avoid building your mounds is under trees, because tree roots will seek out the nutrient-rich soil and the moisture. Nearby trees may also reduce the amount of direct sunlight that falls on your garden. That doesn't mean, however, that trees can't serve a purpose in your garden. Native Americans would occasionally leave one tree in the middle of their fields to use for shade and serve as a garden watch station.[20]

When choosing a location, you want to protect your crops from constantly wet soil. The very nature of growing your crops on a raised mound can protect them, but you still want to seek out dryer locations if possible. Mound gardens are durable and can survive harsh rain, but you don't want the area you choose to flood or easily accumulate standing water during periods of intense rainfall.

Strong winds can wreak havoc on your garden by tearing and dehydrating tender leaves. That's why it's ideal to place your garden on the upper end of a sloping hill, preferably south facing since the bottom of hills can accumulate cold, sinking air in the fall and early spring. The Hidatsa Indians learned that their east-facing slopes experienced less frost than their west-facing slopes.[21] They also noticed that the lowest areas in their fields would experience more frost, while their west-facing fields had less elevation than the east-facing fields.

THE NATIVE AMERICAN WAY

The Native American tribes of the past would build a little platform in the middle of their garden so that they could always have someone watching their crops. Women and children would sing songs and play games at this platform, thus scaring away animal pests. They also believed that their crops loved the singing and grew larger and quicker due to the extra attention and love.[22]

Source: Caduto and Bruchac, *Native American Gardening*, 52.

Mound Orientation

If you plan on growing crops of different heights, you will typically want to choose an east-west orientation and plant the tallest crops on the north end of that mound. You can choose a north-south orientation if most of your crops are the same height. The goal is to prevent the shading of shorter crops unless there is a need to keep seasonal crops cooler when it starts to get hotter in the summer.

Mound Spacing

Typically, mounds are placed three to five feet apart to prevent disease and weeds and to reduce watering demands. That was the norm in the Native American garden, as harmful effects had been observed when the mounds were planted closer than three feet apart.[23] However, it also depended on which crops were grown. The Hidatsa Indians often said that corn would "smell each other" when the mounds were planted too close, and as a result, there would be fewer and smaller corn kernels.[24,25]

The amount of rainfall in your region will also dictate mound spacing. If rainfall is scarce, for example, the mounds should have more spacing between them. If you plan to rely only on rainfall for watering your garden, then space your mounds accordingly.

EXPERT TIP

You'll want to avoid soil compaction at all costs, so make sure you give yourself enough room because you should *never* walk on your garden mounds. Refer to the appropriate chapters for any specifications for the individual mound types.

Sunlight

Sunlight gives your crops the energy they require to produce a good yield and to maintain a healthy and consistent growth phase. It's very important that your garden gets a minimum of six to eight hours of direct sunlight. Plants collect the sun's energy throughout the day and utilize the stored energy for growth at night. Proper sunlight can make the difference between mediocre results and bountiful yields.

The typical garden includes plants such as tomatoes, peppers, corn, squash, and cucumbers, all of which grow best with many hours of direct sunlight. Early morning sunlight with some shading by late afternoon is best, as it also allows the morning dew and any water-sprayed leaves to dry out before nightfall, thus preventing some fungal infections. Keep in mind that there is such a thing as too much sun. Late afternoon shading allows your more delicate plants to get some reprieve if air temperatures are extremely high.

☼ EXPERT TIP

Make sure that you take into account that the sun rises and sets lower in the sky as the growing season progresses into fall and winter. This translates into reduced sunlight strength. More shading may occur, and this may affect the amount of direct sunlight hours. You will have more flexibility with your leaf crops, such as lettuces and kales.

Watering Devices

Proper watering helps develop roots while preventing fungal infections and plant diseases. One lesson that's important to learn from the ancients is how to make it easier on yourself. Just as you don't want to plant in an area that is prone to flooding, you also don't want to be toting gallons of water to the far end of your yard. Here are two common devices you can utilize to water your garden:

→ Olla: This is a low temperature–fired clay vase or bowl. Because it's fired at a low temperature, when you put water in the vase, the clay gets damp and the water seeps out slowly. If you bury the olla in your garden up to the rim and continually fill it with water, that water will slowly seep into the ground where the crops need it most—at the roots. This allows you to water more effectively and efficiently, while also cutting down on weeds, because the soil surface isn't wet.

→ Drip system: This system requires that you hook up equipment to your outdoor faucet or watering source. It's like an olla, but aboveground. Picture a hose that winds through your garden and slowly releases water through little pores. You can put devices like these on timers so that they water your crops a couple of times a day.

One of the biggest mistakes that I ever made when gardening was not utilizing watering devices. Given where I was in Northern Virginia, the crops were so thirsty in the summer that the harvest would suffer from watering issues. I learned the importance of watering devices from this mistake.

A good rule of thumb to follow is that any plants with fruiting bodies will require more water, but in general, all plants (except for cactus and some herbs) like consistently moist soil. Avoid extremes; it's not that your plants won't be able to tolerate some drying out but avoid going from super dry to wet. If you've ever seen a tomato with a black spot on the bottom, that comes from inconsistent watering. The calcium can't get to the cells of that area, which makes the cell walls rot.

In the next chapter, we'll explore types of crops, including some New World and some Old World crops that you can grow in your newly built mound gardens. There are so many crops available for you to grow, but we will delve into the most familiar. Though we'll concentrate on vegetables, don't let this stop you from researching and growing berries and fruits.

CHAPTER 6

NEW WORLD AND OLD WORLD CROPS: WHICH TO GROW?

"When a man moves away from nature, his heart becomes hard."
—Lakota proverb[26]

I t's time to figure out which crops you want to plant in your mound garden. Thinking about all the possibilities can be overwhelming, so here is a quick checklist that can help you narrow down your options while giving you a better chance of success.

1. Grow appropriate crops for your area, but also choose plants that you love eating. There is no sense in growing crops that will just sit on your counter or in the fridge.

2. Once you have a list of plants that you would like to grow, you can find out through programs in your county—like the Master Gardener program or the Cooperative Extension System—which varieties will grow best in your area and climate. Where I live in Virginia, we have a CFC Farm and Home Center, which sells supplies to farmers and can also serve as a useful guide. Resources will differ depending on where you live, but they are out there.

3. To increase your chances of success, choose crop varieties that are drought, disease, or heat tolerant. These crops are usually hybrids with disease protection.

4. If you want to collect seeds for subsequent plantings, you will need to choose open-pollinated varieties.

5. If possible, select two varieties of a specific vegetable, just in case one does not do so well.

6. Grow crops that are not only rugged and low maintenance, but also have a long shelf life. This allows you to grow a lot of the crop and create a steady food supply. A good example is Seminole pumpkins, which can last on your counter for over a year.

7. Do not overplant the mound. Follow seed package guidelines or the mound-specific guidelines discussed in the following chapters.

8. Plant extra amounts to compensate for losses due to animals, insects, and disease.

THE NATIVE AMERICAN WAY

The Native American tribes of the past kept a few varieties of corn seeds that grew well in different locations and under different weather conditions. They planned ahead for possible crop failures.

Source: William Moys Weaver, "Native American Gardening," Mother Earth News, accessed December 6, 2020, https://www.motherearthnews.com/organic-gardening/vegetables/native-american-gardening-zm0z13fmzsto.

NEW WORLD CROPS

New World crops are those common to the Americas and utilized by various Native American tribes throughout history. The following list provides detailed characteristics for each of these crops.

→ **CORN**: The corn plant is the queen of the crop. A major staple of the Native American tribes of the past,[27] corn continues to feed multitudes of people. Corn also performs a major support function in a polyculture garden by acting like a pole for your beans to grow up.

- Ease of Growth: Medium.

- Level of Demand: Medium.

- Season: Warm.

- Growing: Sow seeds about one-and-a-half to two inches deep and space out four to six inches apart. Provide full sun (six to eight hours) and consistently moist, rich organic soil. Corn grows well in nitrogen-rich soil.

- Potential Issues: Almost no issues except for corn worms.

- Harvesting: Harvest when a squeezed kernel squirts out white milky juice. You should be able to start testing after the silk starts turning brown.

→ **PEPPERS**: Related to tomatoes, peppers can be one of your most prolific crops. You can grow sweet, mildly spicy, or hot peppers. You can eat the fruit green or let them turn to their final color of red, purple, or yellow.

  - Ease of Growth: Medium.

  - Level of Demand: Medium.

  - Season: Warm.

  - Growing: Start peppers indoors to maximize the size and age of the plant before replanting outdoors after the last frost. Sow seeds about one-half inch deep and space out 18 to 24 inches when seedlings are replanted outdoors. Provide full sun (minimum six to eight hours) and moist, preferably rich organic soil. Peppers are heavy feeders and like a consistently moist soil and warm temperatures.

  - Potential Issues: Almost no issues.

  - Harvesting: Harvest when fruits are large and ripe. Certain varieties are meant to be allowed to turn red for the best flavor.

→ **WINTER SQUASH:** This crop is one of the noble sisters in a Native American Three Sisters garden,[28] which will be described in detail in the chapter on Native American mounds. Some of these squash types look no different than the common field pumpkin but taste much sweeter and are much more rugged in growth and pest resistance. Why not have your own pumpkin patch?

- Ease of Growth: Easy.

- Level of Demand: Medium.

- Season: Warm.

- Growing: Start squash indoors to maximize the size and age of the plant before replanting outdoors after the last frost. Sow seeds about one inch deep. Provide full sun (six to eight hours) and consistently moist, rich organic soil. Keep covered with row covers when plants are young. Remove row covers when plants are flowering, or you will need to hand fertilize.

- Potential Issues: You may have some issues with squash bugs, vine borers, and powdery mildew. Go with the *C. moschata* subspecies, as it is more resistant to the above-mentioned pests and will get only minor infestations of them.

- Harvesting: Typical harvesting occurs when you can indent the skin of the squash only slightly with your fingernail. A bonus is that the young green squash can be harvested and will often taste like zucchini. The leaves and growing tips can be eaten, too. Mature squash can last for many months on your countertop, even up to a year and a half if properly cured and of the right variety.

→ **SUNCHOKES** (a.k.a. Jerusalem artichokes): This crop wins one of the grand prizes for ease of growth and immense pest resistance. This plant fed many Native Americans and can be easily grown for the delicious edible root bulbs it produces.[29]

You can even leave the bulbs in the ground and dig them up in the middle of a harsh winter when you want to make a rich sunchoke soup.

- Ease of Growth: Easy.

- Level of Demand: Low.

- Season: Warm.

- Growing: Sow root bulbs about two to three inches deep. Provide full sun (six to eight hours) and moist, rich organic soil.

- Potential Issues: Few issues with this flower, but it can become almost invasive.

- Harvesting: Typical harvesting consists of digging up the bulbs as needed. Any bulbs or pieces you leave will sprout the next year, so be prepared for a constant food source.

→ **BEANS:** Another sibling in the Three Sisters garden,[30] beans can be one of your most productive crops with the added benefit that they fertilize your mounds with nitrogen. Pole beans will require a pole or trellis to climb, where bush beans will typically form a small self-standing bush.

- Ease of Growth: Easy.

- Level of Demand: Low to medium.

- Season: Warm.

- Growing: Start beans indoors to maximize the size and age of the plant before replanting outdoors after the last frost. Sow seeds no deeper than one to one-and-a-half inches and space plants out to about four inches apart. Provide full sun (six to eight hours) and moist, preferably medium-rich organic soil. Beans will do best in soil with medium to slightly lower nitrogen levels. Adding nitrogen fixing powder to the bean seed before planting will benefit plant growth.

- Potential Issues: Mexican bean beetles can be a nuisance.

- Harvesting: For best flavor, pick beans when they are young and small. For beans that can survive storage, harvest the bean pods when the plant's vigor appears to be fading and it starts losing many of its older leaves. Extract the beans from the pods and air-dry for a minimum of three days. After your beans have dried, I recommend storing them in airtight jars. Drying your beans will allow a very long storage life for this vertical, fast-growing wonder crop.

→ **TOMATOES:** Probably the most popular crop of all—and once considered poisonous—the tomato is a joy to grow. The juiciness and luscious taste of an heirloom tomato is unrivaled if you like tomatoes. You can grow two different types of tomato plants.

- Determinate: These tomato plants grow like a bush to a set height and typically produce one large harvest.

- Indeterminate: These plants grow taller in a vine-like form and will produce tomatoes until the plant dies or succumbs to frost.

- Ease of Growth: Medium.

- Level of Demand: Medium.

- Season: Warm.

- Growing: Start tomatoes indoors to maximize the size and age of the plant before replanting outdoors after the last frost. Sow seeds no deeper than one-quarter to one-half inch and space plants out to about 24 inches apart. Provide full sun (minimum six to eight hours) and moist, preferably rich organic soil. Tomatoes are heavy feeders and like a consistently moist soil and warm temperatures. Make sure to stake up indeterminate tomatoes, as they can get very tall. Tomato plants love lots of airflow and plenty of consistent watering for optimal growth.

- Potential Issues: Tomato hornworms and blights.

- Harvesting: Harvest when fruits are mostly red and ripe, and then allow them to finish ripening on your counter. If allowed to overripen on the vine, there is the chance that the fruit will be nipped at or cracked.

OLD WORLD CROPS

These are crops that, over millennia, have become staples for the people of Europe, Asia, and Africa.

→ **CABBAGE:** This is one of the healthiest and most nutrient-rich crops to grow. The Romans considered cabbage a luxury crop and also used it medicinally for headaches, gout, and preventing hangovers.[31] One good thing about growing cabbage is that you can get a second harvest after cutting off the main head and letting the side heads regrow.

- Ease of Growth: Medium.

- Level of Demand: Medium.

- Season: Cool.

- Growing: You can start cabbage indoors about four to six weeks before the last frost to maximize the size and age of the plant, and then replant outdoors a few weeks before the last frost. If planting from seed, sow the seeds no deeper than one-quarter to one-half inch and space plants out to about 18 to 24 inches apart as soon as the soil can be worked. Provide full sun and cool temperatures for optimal growth. Keep covered with row covers or else be prepared to pick off cabbage worms. A weekly spraying of BT (*Bacillus thuringiensis*) or consistent picking of any caterpillars may be required.

- Potential Issues: Not many issues except for cabbage worms.

- Harvesting: Harvest when heads are large and firm.

→ **ARUGULA** (a.k.a. rocket): Arugula is another ancient food plant that was also used as a companion plant by the Romans to protect other crops from pests. Arugula was considered an aphrodisiac by the ancients.[32] The spicy nature of this plant adds zing to salads and a milder taste when sautéed.

- Ease of Growth: Easy.

- Level of Demand: Low to medium.

- Season: Cool.

- Growing: Plant a couple of weeks before the last frost date. Sow seeds no deeper than one-eighth to one-quarter inch and space plants out to about 12 inches apart. Provide full sun and cool temperatures for optimal growth. Keep covered with row covers if needed for protection. This plant can remain dormant throughout winter if covered with straw or mulch before a freeze sets in. Remove the mulch in early spring to continue growth and harvesting.

- Potential Issues: Not many issues.

- Harvesting: The youngest leaves are the most flavorful and mild. Continuously harvesting the outer leaves is the best way to utilize this old diehard crop. Don't pick more than half the plant so that you can give it some time to regrow in between.

→ **TURNIP:** Turnips are a cool season crop that has the benefit of edible leaves and roots. The leaves can be sautéed or stewed. The root can be boiled, baked, or roasted. On a historical note, turnips were used as jack-o'-lanterns in Europe, centuries before pumpkins became the standard.[33] Just use caution when carving, as this vegetable is very hard and requires a lot of force to cut through.

- Ease of Growth: Medium.

- Level of Demand: Medium.

- Season: Cool.

- Growing: Plant a couple of weeks before the last frost date. Sow seeds no deeper than one-half inch and space plants out to about four inches apart. Provide full sun and cool temperatures for optimal growth. One to two inches of water a week should more than suffice for this popular root vegetable.

- Potential Issues: Not many issues. Very low chance of insect, pest, fungal, or other disease issues.

- Harvesting: Continuously harvest some of the outer leaves or wait for the root to get large enough (up to three inches in diameter) but not to full size.

→ **BEETS:** Beets are a cool season crop that have the benefit of edible leaves and roots. This crop has also been used medicinally by the Romans, Greeks, and Egyptians to benefit digestive health.[34]

- Ease of Growth: Easy.

- Level of Demand: Low.

- Season: Cool.

- Growing: Plant a couple of weeks before the last frost date. Sow seeds no deeper than one-half inch and space plants out to about two inches apart. Provide full sun and cool temperatures for optimal growth.

- Potential Issues: Not many issues.

- Harvesting: Continuously harvest some of the outer leaves or wait for the root to get large enough (up to two inches in diameter) but not to full size.

→ **LETTUCE:** Lettuce is a cool season crop that should be a staple in your garden. It is so easy and fast to grow that there should be no reason to buy bags of it. The Egyptians, Greeks, and Romans all loved lettuce for the digestive and sedative-like properties of the sap at the plant's base. This is possibly the reason the Romans named it "lactuca," which means milk.[35]

- Ease of Growth: Easy.

- Level of Demand: Low.

- Season: Cool.

- Growing: Lettuce can be planted in mid to later spring for best results. Sow seeds no deeper than one-quarter to one-half inch and space plants out to about six inches apart. Provide full sun and cool temperatures for optimal growth. Lettuce grows best with consistently moist soil and increased shading when the late spring and early summer heat kicks in. Keep covered with row covers for optimal protection if needed.

- Potential Issues: Not many issues except for keeping the plant cool and its shallow roots protected with mulch.

- Harvesting: Continuously harvesting the outer leaves is the best way to utilize this crop. Just don't pick more than half of the plant; give it some time to regrow in between.

→ **RED ORACH:** Red orach was possibly the original spinach and was well known and loved during antiquity. The Greeks, Romans, and much of ancient Europe loved the flavor of the beautiful red and purplish leaves.[36] It hails from weed-like ancestors, as evidenced by the durability of this plant. It can survive some light freezes and can tolerate somewhat warm temperatures.

- Ease of Growth: Easy.

- Level of Demand: Low to medium.

- Season: Cool or warm.

- Growing: Plant a week or two after the last frost date. Sow seeds no deeper than one-half inch and space plants out to about 10–12 inches apart. Provide full sun (six to eight hours) and consistently moist, moderately rich soil for the best results.

- Potential Issues: May have some issues with caterpillars or aphids

- Harvesting: Keep this plant trimmed down, as it can reach five to six feet tall. Try to continuously harvest before it sets seed by picking off any flowers that appear to be forming.

→ **SWISS CHARD:** Swiss chard is a very colorful leafy crop with some varieties being yellow, red, and bright orange. This plant is quite easy to grow and relatively pest-free. Every garden should have at least a few swiss chard plants, even if only for their beauty.

- Ease of Growth: Easy.

- Level of Demand: Low.

- Season: Cool or warm.

- Growing: Plant a couple of weeks before the last frost date. Sow seeds no deeper than one-half inch and space plants out to about four to six inches apart. Provide full sun (six to eight hours) and consistently moist soil for the best results. The adult plant can remain dormant throughout winter if covered with straw or mulch before a freeze sets in. Remove the mulch in early spring for continued growth and harvesting.

- Potential Issues: May have some issues with slugs or caterpillars.

- Harvesting: Continuously harvesting the outer leaves is the best way to utilize this old diehard crop. Just don't pick more than half of the plant; give it some time to regrow in between.

→ **ONION:** Onion greens and bulbs likely originated in Asia and have been enjoyed by humans for thousands of years in both Asia and Europe.[37] They come in mild varieties, such as the sweet onion, and in very strong varieties.

- Ease of Growth: Easy.

- Level of Demand: Low.

- Season: Cool.

- Growing: Onions are typically planted in the early spring as soon as the ground is soft and loose enough to be worked. Plant onion bulbs at about two inches deep and space them out about two to three inches apart. Onion seeds should be planted about one-half inch deep with the same spacing as the bulbs. Provide full sun (six to eight hours) and consistently moist soil with a light mulch to retain the soil moisture.

- Potential Issues: Not many issues.

- Harvesting: Onions should be harvested when the plant's aboveground leaves fall over and turn brown, but they can be harvested at any phase of their growth.

→ **CUCUMBER:** Native to India, the juicy cucumber was well known to the Greeks, the Romans, and the Egyptians. The Roman Emperor Tiberius had his own mobile cucumber garden.[38] This is how well loved this ancient vegetable was to many in antiquity.

- Ease of Growth: Medium.

- Level of Demand: Medium.

- Season: Warm.

- Growing: Start growing cucumbers indoors to maximize the size and age of the plant before replanting outdoors at least a couple weeks after the last frost. Sow seeds about one to two inches deep. Provide full sun (six to eight hours) and consistently moist, rich organic soil. Keep covered with row covers when plants are young. Remove row covers when plants are flowering, or you will need to hand fertilize.

- Potential Issues: May have some issues with squash bugs, cucumber beetles, slugs, aphids, and powdery mildew. Try not to pick cucumbers or handle the plants just after a rain, as wet leaves will be the most susceptible to powdery mildews.

- Harvesting: Typical harvesting occurs with smaller cucumber fruit, as they grow very fast and can get bitter.

→ **CARROT:** Carrots are an old-time favorite root vegetable that harbors great quantities of beta carotene.[39]

- Ease of Growth: Easy.

- Level of Demand: Low.

- Season: Cool.

- Growing: Carrots are typically planted about three to four weeks before last frost. Plant your carrot seeds at about one-quarter inch deep and space them out about two to three inches apart. Provide full sun (six to eight hours) and consistently moist soil.

- Potential Issues: Rocky soil will cause malformed carrots.

ENHANCE YOUR EXPERIENCE

Take notes about what you planted, when you planted, harvest dates, and what is currently blooming or hatching. Simple notes are fine; this shouldn't be a chore. Hopefully, you will have an overwhelming desire to build many types of mound gardens. If so, these notes will provide you with ideas for not only multiple types of gardens, but also hybrid forms that will make your new hobby more enjoyable and more productive.

COMPANION CROPS

Certain crops make better neighbors than others. When in doubt, a good rule of thumb is to not plant crops from the same family together, such as potatoes and tomatoes, because they make for bad growing partners. For example, one crop might be susceptible to a disease and could transfer that disease to the other crop. Sometimes, even crops from different families can make poor growing partners, like kale and strawberries, because roots from one crop can exude certain chemicals that aren't tolerated by the other crops.

Following is a simple, go-to list you can reference when deciding which crops you want to plant in your mound garden.

TOMATOES:

→ Good Companions: Onion, parsley, carrots, celery, lettuce, and spinach.

→ Bad Companions: Cabbage, peas, potatoes, and beets.

BEANS:

→ Good Companions: Corn and plants from the cabbage and squash families.

→ Bad Companions: Beets and plants from the onion family.

CORN:

→ Good Companions: Plants from the bean and squash families.

→ Bad Companions: Plants from the tomato family.

CABBAGE:

→ Good Companions: Plants from the bean family.

→ Bad Companions: Plants from the tomato family.

CUCUMBERS:

→ Good Companions: Celery, corn, lettuce, peas, radishes, and plants from the bean family.

→ Bad Companions: Melons, potatoes, and aromatic herbs.

PEPPERS:

→ Good Companions: Tomatoes, lettuce, and plants from the onion family.

→ Bad Companions: Potatoes and plants from the cabbage and bean families.

OTHER PLANTING TECHNIQUES

You can create a very fruitful and productive garden by utilizing strategies that have helped the ancients survive over the millennia. Two of these strategies include the following:

→ Intercropping: This will allow you to maximize your yield by planting smaller crops that mature faster in the unused space on your mound that would eventually be used by the mound's main crop. You can then continue to grow these crops on the perimeters of the mounds as your main crop fills the center regions. Just make sure you plant sun loving companions on the southern edges of the mound as the main crop may eventually block sunlight from these companion plants. A wise intercropping strategy is to use nitrogen-fixing crops (legumes) as one of your main crop's mound partners.

→ Succession Planting: This is the process of spacing out the planting times of one crop so that you get multiple harvests and not one big harvest. This will allow you to enjoy a steady supply of one of your favorite crops as each batch matures and becomes harvestable.

Before you start digging into the ground, measure out your planned garden at the prospective site and plan your garden on paper first, if possible. The ancients would mark out the areas with stakes, stones, or little earth mounds.[40] Perform your final checks on the amount of sunlight, quality of soil, and other important factors that can increase your chances of a healthy garden and a great harvest.

THE SEMINOLE PUMPKIN

I had no idea how much I loved the Seminole pumpkin until I started growing it in my mound garden. It's not that I didn't like it before, but I have grown to love it and have since grown tons of them. They are the perfect food for storing because they can last for a year and a half if you store them properly. Regular pumpkins don't come close to lasting that long, and though the Seminole pumpkin is actually a squash, even squash won't last that long. Butternut squash may last a year, but the Seminole pumpkin far surpasses that. These are, by far, my favorite crops to grow!

You can grow a lot of pumpkins in your mound garden. You might get five pumpkins per vine and have three vines per mound. So, if you have five mounds, that's 75 pumpkins. These pumpkins are all over my house. I probably have had at times 50 two- to three-pound pumpkins in my basement from a previous summer. I keep one on each corner of my desk at work, and people come by to ask me about them all the time. I tell them the story of how the indigenous Seminole tribe in Florida survived on these hundreds of years ago, but they actually grew and stored them up trees.[41] They couldn't bury their food in Florida because of the water level.

In my house, we use the Seminole pumpkins to make pumpkin soup and pumpkin fritters. We roast them, microwave them, and steam them. When you eat them green, they taste like zucchini. If you let them age, they taste a little sweeter than butternut squash. You can eat the leaves, seeds, and points off the main vine. You can even batter up the buds before the flower opens. The entire plant is edible and can be used.

The next six chapters delve into the various types of mound gardens that can be built and their varying levels of complexity. You get to choose which style best suits you. I am hoping you will build all of them over time.

CHAPTER 7

SURVIVAL MOUND GARDENS

"If you are planning for a year, sow rice; if you are planning for a decade, plant trees; if you are planning for a lifetime, educate people."
—Guan Zhong[42]

I f another pandemic occurs and grocery store shelves are cleared out, you don't want to be stuck short on food. We all saw what happened to food and supplies when people were asked to self-quarantine in March 2020. It's during times like those when a survival garden comes in handy.

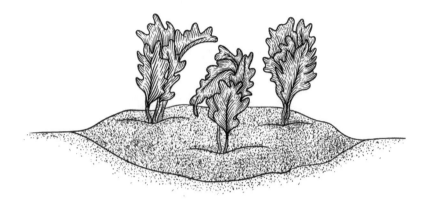

Let's start with the basics, and it doesn't get any more basic than the survival mound. This garden is simply a mound built on top of loosened, enriched soil and compostable material mix. It's one of the least expensive forms of gardening when it comes to material and labor.

Mound gardening isn't just an ancient practice. Modern-day survivalists have learned to plant survival mounds, because they increase the chances of a healthy crop by providing the benefits of a well-fertilized, raised, and deep grow area. Other mound variations enhance crop growth and production without the addition of costly fertilizers or constant watering.

Benefits:

→ The survival mound is one of the quickest mounds to build.

→ This mound is also one of the quickest ways to utilize small batches of kitchen scraps and yard waste.

Specifications:

→ Mound Height: Typically, four inches.

→ Mound Width: Typically, 16–20 inches in diameter.

→ Depth: 12 or more inches deep.

→ Spacing: Typically, four to five feet between mound centers, but during drought conditions the spacing can be increased to six to eight feet.

The Process:

1. Choose a proper location for the garden, ideally in the fall or winter before the garden is planted.

2. Dig a hole in your selected location, a minimum of 16 inches in diameter and 12 inches deep. Place high-nutrient plant or animal wastes at the bottom of the hole and fill the hole about halfway. Continue filling the hole with either purchased soilless mix, raised-bed mix, pure compost, or a known rich and healthy soil.

3. Build a mound on top about four inches high. Level and then plant on top of the mound. You can form a circular rim of soil on the top of the mound to capture and hold more water.

4. De-weed and loosen the spaces between the mounds later. It is not critical to have the spaces between your mounds weed free or the soil loosened at planting time as the mound structures themselves will provide your new crops with these attributes. The in-between mound weeding and soil loosening can also be done naturally and labor free by laying down and maintaining a thick layer of mulch.

5. Perform a soil compaction and soil consistency test as described in Chapter 3, so you can resolve any compaction or soil consistency issues before you plant.

For Best Results:

→ Plant easy, low-demand crops at first. Higher-demand crops will struggle unless the soil is rich enough to support their higher nutrient demands.

→ Space the mounds to utilize only rainfall.

→ With proper fertilizing, subsequent crops can be of the higher-demand types.

→ Utilize cover crops and organic nutrients on those mounds as they lie dormant. The goal is to enrich the soil while it lies unused with compost mulch, cover crops, compost teas, organic fertilizers, or soil amendments.

→ A biweekly use of free liquid fertilizers such as compost tea, weed teas, or diluted urine will ensure that extra nutrients are available for your crops. Spraying your plants with compost tea will not only fertilize your plants but will also lend protection from some fungal diseases.

→ Typically, plant two to three crops, equally spaced, per mound.

My Personal Experience:

When constructing my own survival mounds, I dig a hole and bury my tea bags, coffee grounds and other kitchen scraps. I used to go to Starbucks to get their coffee grounds, but don't go as much anymore because people beat me to it in the morning. Since I got rid of my compost bin, I have started putting my food waste in my survival mounds. That has proven to be the easiest way to get rid of my waste and have a garden at the same time. I typically plant pumpkins and other crops that thrive in compost or a base of yard waste, tea bags, coffee grounds, and food waste.

THE NATIVE AMERICAN WAY

For survival reasons, Native American tribes of the past would take advantage of any edible weeds that grew in their gardens. Why give up free nutrition and access to very hardy plants? Some of the most common edible weeds found in today's yards and gardens are:

→ Mullein

→ Red clover

→ Yarrow

→ Plantain

→ Nettle

Grow a few of these weedy perennials in your mound garden. Every gardener should have at least one survival mound in their yard, as it is one of the simplest gardening options to practice.

Source: V. Havard, "Food Plants of the North American Indians," *Bulletin of the Torrey Botanical Club* 22, no. 3 (1895): 98-123, https://doi.org/10.2307/2477757.

CHAPTER 8

NATIVE AMERICAN MOUND GARDENS

"So long as the three sisters are with us, we know we will never starve."
—Chief Louis Farmer, Onondaga Tribe[43]

A **few years ago,** my best friend Billy, who I had known for over
40 years, passed away from lung cancer. He was part Native
American. His grandfather was a Cayuga descendent, which
was one of the six nations of the Haudenosaunee Confederacy, along
with the Seneca, Onondaga, Oneida, Mohawk, and the Tuscarora.[44]
The Confederacy is an alliance of Native Nations residing in the New
York area.

When Billy and I were young, I used to love going over to his grandparents' house and listening to his grandfather tell stories. That was when I first started to learn and appreciate Native American cultures, and that reverence has stayed with me throughout my adult life. Now that I'm older, I really appreciate their ingenuity when it comes to gardening—their culture depends on being able to grow their own food.

Not only have I fallen in love with many of the crops they grew in order to survive, but I've also developed my own ceremonial practices to pay tribute to those tribal cultures that first utilized these gardening techniques. When traveling through Tennessee and North Carolina, I stopped at the various reservations and purchased Cherokee bowls and other authentic Native American pottery. Over the years, I have used those bowls during my daily gardening routines. I put my seeds in a bowl and carry it out to the garden. Throughout the garden, I lay out commemorative arrowheads and rocks that I got from those tribal areas, and they help to create an almost magical atmosphere. For me, it is more of a meditation—I feel the wind and just say, "Thank you."

THE HISTORY

During my research over the years, it became clear to me that the Native American tribes of the past utilized mound gardening techniques, in one form or another, more than any of the other ancient cultures. Theses tribes learned that mounds allowed them to plant earlier in the growing season and create a slightly longer growing season. They preferred building their gardens on a floodplain, since the soil is usually very rich due to river floods depositing nutrient-bearing silts.[45] Starting your Native American mound garden with very rich soil is therefore imperative.

This form of gardening didn't rely on extensive plowing or disturbance of the soil like the European style of farming, which is now known to decrease soil fertility. First, all cleared brush and trees would be burned on the actual mound sites. This would soften and loosen the soil, making the task of building the mounds much easier with the benefit of adding calcium and other nutrients. A digging stick and hoe were the principal tools that were used to first loosen the soil and then hoe the soil into mounds.

DID YOU KNOW?

Centuries ago, Native American maize farmers in east-central North America produced three to five times as much grain as European wheat farmers.

Source: David J. Tenenbaum, "Farming, Native American Style," The Why? Files, April 5, 2012, https://whyfiles.org/2012/farming-native-american-style/index.html.

Native American farmers typically built flat-topped mounds of soil used to cluster their crops throughout a growing area. They had learned that small clusters of plants grew better than long rows of plants due to the actual environmental conditions within a grouping of plants. Polyculture, or the practice of growing multiple crops in the same spot, was often used by these farmers, as they had noticed the numerous benefits of growing certain crops in proximity of each other. They let the strengths of each plant benefit the others.[46]

THE NATIVE AMERICAN WAY

Native Americans would often sing and think positive thoughts while in their mound gardens. In addition to the singing scaring away any critters, they believed that singing and positive thoughts would induce a great harvest that growing season. Quarreling in the garden or about the garden could bring on bad luck for the harvest.

BUILDING YOUR MOUND

Benefits:

→ No tilling is required, which will keep the soil fertile and healthy.

→ This method utilizes companion planting, which creates a symbiotic relationship that benefits all of the plants in the mound.

→ Enhances population-density control.

→ Reduces soil erosion.

→ Provides protection from excessive rainfall and the damage of wet roots during cooler weather.

Specifications:

→ Mound Height: Typically, three to four inches.

→ Mound Width: Typically, 12–18 inches in diameter with a 10-inch flat base on top depending on the type of seeds planted.

→ These mounds can be up to 36 inches in diameter.

→ Spacing: Allow four to five feet between mound centers in usual conditions but increase in drought conditions to six to eight feet apart.

In addition to starting their gardens on very rich floodplain soil, Native Americans utilized the nitrogen-fixing properties of beans along with occasional wood ash treatments to fertilize the soil. You can use pit compost areas to build on, and you can also bury minor amounts of fish waste or pour diluted urine into the soil about a foot under the mound if you want to utilize a few composting techniques that Native American tribes were believed to have used in the past.[47] As with survival mounds, it is best to add a two- to three-inch top-dressing layer of compost at the end of the growing season. This layer of compost emulates the river deposits that enriched the soil in garden locations typically used by these tribes.

♀ EXPERT TIP

For a genuine experience and to honor the Native American tribes of the past, try to replicate their gardening techniques to a T. This would involve polyculture and following specific tribes' planting formats, etc.

The Process:

1. Choose a proper location for the garden. Ideally, this should be done in the fall or winter before the garden is planted. Mark off the mound locations with rocks or wooden stakes.

2. Loosen the onsite rich soil with digging sticks or utilize purchased soil or raised-bed mixes. It is very important that the soil is dark, nutrient rich, and friable. If grass is present in your selected area, cut into the grass turf and remove. Place this cut piece of turf into the bottom of your compost pile or pit. You can burn weeds or other yard waste on top of the mound areas to soften and fertilize at the same time. Just don't add too much ash, as this will make the mound area very alkaline.

3. Build mounds with wider bases and narrower tops. Create rows with three to four feet or more space between mound centers.

4. De-weed and loosen the spaces between the mounds at a later time. Enlarge your garden later by building additional mounds following the spacing criteria used earlier.

5. Utilize diluted urine, compost teas, or organic liquid fertilizers until the planted legumes can provide nitrogen to the mounds.

For Best Results:

→ Utilize polyculture or any of the other companion plant pairings listed in Chapter 6.

→ Consider that some crops germinate and grow better on the side of the mounds, as with beans in a corn and bean mound.

→ Follow tested spacing specifications or seed package guidelines.

→ Grow multiple varieties of the same crop. This should ensure that you get a decent harvest even when one variety might not perform as well.

→ Let the mounds lie fallow after about three years of use. Continue to utilize cover crops and organic nutrients on those mounds as they lie dormant. The goal is to enrich the soil while it lies unused.

DID YOU KNOW?

The Hopi Indians believed that the sound of the wind
rustling through the leaves of the trees and crops was the gods
speaking to them.

Source: "Fremont's Cottonwood," United States Department of Agriculture Natural
Resources Conservation Service, December 5, 2000, https://plants.usda.gov/plantguide/
pdf/cs_pofr2.pdf.

THE THREE SISTERS

When I built my first Native American mound, I decided to pay tribute
to those rich cultures by planting the Three Sisters. Native American
tribes learned to plant their three main crops together in one mound as
companion plants because they fed off each other. Those three plants are:

1. Corn.

2. Beans.

3. Squash.[48]

The corn is planted first. When it reaches seven to 12 inches, plant the
beans, which grow much faster. Beans are trellising plants that wrap
around the corn, which literally becomes a bean pole. Beans also pull
nitrogen out of the air and store it on their nodules and in their roots.
They add nitrogen to the soil right next to the corn, which is a heavy
nitrogen feeder. The squash is planted third because it crawls close to the
ground while it grows, as opposed to the other two that grow upward.
The squash gets its nitrogen from the beans while also shading the ground
to prevent water loss and evaporation. The wide and prickly leaves of the

squash repel animals like racoons. Together, these three crops have the perfect symbiotic relationship and serve as excellent companion plants.

What I have always found so interesting was how gardens became a knowledge system of sorts for Native Americans. The songs and stories about the Three Sisters and their other crops became intertwined with their cultural lives.[49]

WHERE DO YOU LIVE?

Native American mound gardening is best suited for those living east of the Mississippi River because of the increased rainfall, while a depressed mound is better suited for those living west of the Mississippi. You can certainly build Native American mounds if you live west of the Mississippi, but you might need an olla or another watering device because they potentially dry out quicker.

CHAPTER 9

HÜGELKULTUR MOUND GARDENS

"A society grows great when old men plant trees whose shade they know they shall never sit in."
—Proverb

Hügelkultur mound gardening techniques have been practiced in Germany and Eastern Europe for hundreds of years.[50] These mounds work on the principle that a mound with a thick core of rotting wood will feed and provide moisture to your crops for many years.

Hügelkultur is a composting process that involves a mound constructed from decaying wood debris and other compostable biomass plant materials and covered by nutrient-rich soil. This means that you need less soil even though the nutrients are dispersed better than in any other mound, because the process itself helps to improve the soil and water retention. This improves the health of the plants on and even near the mound.

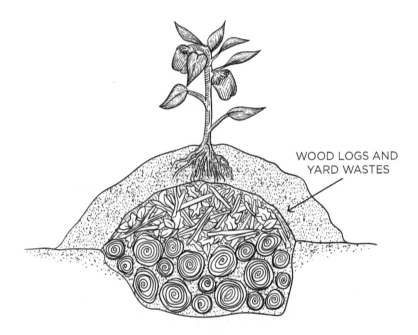

WOOD LOGS AND YARD WASTES

If you choose to add a Hügelkultur mound to your garden, it will probably be one of your largest mounds. Even smaller fruit trees will benefit, thus expanding your choice of food-producing plants. The increased height can provide shade on the north side of the mound when you build it in an east to west direction, thus extending the growing season for your cool-season crops. And since the central wood cavity of the mound will store water and decompose, you greatly reduce your need to water or fertilize the mound.

I have a few small Hügelkultur mounds that are about four feet long, but you can build them up to 80 feet long if you want. I use these mounds to get rid of all the sticks in my yard and the hard waste. I try to utilize all the hardwood and branches that I cut, using them to extend the mound. That's what's great about this mound type—you can get rid of your yard waste while feeding your plants for years. It's more of a long-duration, less-maintenance type of mound, and that's why I encourage others to utilize this mound type.

DID YOU KNOW?

Hügelkultur can be thought of as a great way to sequester carbon. Dead trees, branches, and yard waste will be buried and used as plant food instead of being burned or buried in a greenhouse gas releasing landfill.

Benefits:

→ This method provides a long-term plant nutrient source.

→ These mounds increase soil aeration due to the numerous nooks and crannies formed by the wood core.

→ The decaying wood core acts like a sponge by absorbing the extra rainfall and dispersing the water as needed.

→ The mound heats faster and retains heat longer due to mound height and the decomposing wooden core. The mound height also aids in capturing more direct sunlight.

→ Less soil is required as the wooden core takes up much of the size of the mound.

Specifications:

→ Mound Height: Typically, three feet.

→ Mound Width: Typically, three to four feet.

→ Mound Length: Any length is allowed.

→ Mound Orientation: North to south or an east to west orientation if shading is required for certain plants.

The Process:

1. Choose a proper location for the garden.

2. Decide if you will create the core of your Hügelkultur mound above ground or below. If you choose below ground, then dig the pit that you plan to use, lay logs or branch materials in, and compact the material as much as possible. In both cases, fill spaces between wood material with leaves and untreated yard waste and then water the wood pile very well. Avoid using walnut, cedar or other woody materials that either resist decay or have natural plant growth inhibiting chemicals.

3. Create a long mound of topsoil and compost on top of the wood pile.

4. Utilize diluted urine, compost teas, or organic liquid fertilizers until the rotting core can provide nitrogen to the mound.

For Best Results:

→ Don't plant heavy nitrogen feeding plants the first year. The Hügelkultur bed will utilize more of this nutrient as it becomes established, typically two to three years after being built.

→ Try to build your Hügelkultur mound the fall before you intend to plant. This will allow the decomposition process to get a head start.

→ Utilize yard waste, branches, and logs for the core of this mound style.

→ Ensure that your new Hügelkultur mound stays moist. This will speed up the decomposition of the wood core and promote healthy fungal and bacterial life in your mound.

CHAPTER 10

KEYHOLE MOUND GARDENS

"Better to eat vegetables and fear no creditors, than
eat duck and hide from them."
—Yiddish proverb[51]

Keyhole mounds are a newer type of planting system that
is being used to feed many villages in Africa.[52] This system utilizes a composting basket that is built in the middle of the mound and leaches out the composting byproducts into the
soil surrounding it. This makes the mound look like a keyhole when
viewed from above, hence the name.

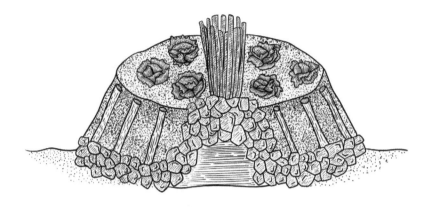

I have a few keyhole mounds built right now and have them planted with lettuce, chard, and other greens. You can grow tomatoes, but this type of mound is tailored for greens. When I'm not burying waste in my survival mound, Native American mound, or where future mounds will be, I throw my tea bags in my keyhole mound. With a keyhole mound, you can put your food scraps and coffee grounds right in the basket during the winter and spring so it will leach into the surrounding part of the mound. I primarily use my keyhole mound to get rid of my waste in the winter. I plan on eventually making larger and more extravagant key-hole mounds.

Benefits:

→ Increased moisture retention.

→ Constant soil-nutrient replenishment.

→ Earlier soil warming.

→ Easier composting.

→ Takes care of composting and fertilizing all at once.

→ A longer gardening season due to the heat output of the center composting basket.

Specifications:

→ Mound Height: Typically, three feet.

→ Mound Width: Typically, five to six feet in diameter.

The Process:

1. Choose a proper location for the garden.

2. Draw a circle five to six feet in diameter. This is a typical size, but your diameter can be smaller if desired.

3. Mark the outline of the garden with the stones or bricks that you will be using.

4. Insert four sticks in the center in the shape of a square.

5. Complete the central basket with rope and thatch grass, or thinner tall sticks.

6. Lay down the first layer of the garden. This can be broken clay shards or small stones.

7. Cover the first layer with a thick layer of compostable material (leaves, dried grass clippings, or food waste). Every subsequent layer should slope downward from the center.

8. Continue to add layers of rich soil and alternate thin layers of completed compost. Continue adding outer stones until the mound reaches the desired height.

For Best Results:

→ Plant leafy and root crops.

→ Utilize companion planting.

→ Keep the composting area of the garden covered when not watering.

CHAPTER 11

RAISED-BED MOUND GARDENS

"We cared for our corn in those days as we care for a child; for we Indian people loved our garden, just as a mother loves her children; and we thought that our growing corn likes to hear us sing, just as children like to hear their mother sing to them."
— Maxidiwiac (Buffalo Bird Woman) Hidatsa[53]

Raised-bed mounds are probably the most familiar type of mound garden to home gardeners. The raised-bed mound is also the most utilized style at schools, churches, and other institutions throughout the world due to the ease of construction and the greater mound height. There are numerous examples of ancient Native American raised-bed mounds (in North and South America), from the

Waru of the Andes,[5455] Chinampas of Mexico,[56] and the mysterious bed mounds of Michigan.[57] This mound style offered the crops of these regions protection from erosion, pests, frost, and drought. In addition to these traditional protections, gardeners with decreased mobility can particularly benefit from the increased height of these mounds and not have to bend so low to the ground.

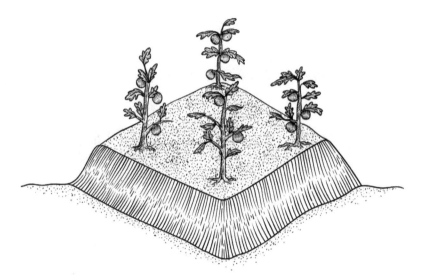

This is the type of mound gardening that I am most familiar with, and most of the raised-bed mounds I've created have been framed. There is the added cost of the material, and slugs and insects can gravitate toward the edge of the frame, but I have found that a frame makes it easier to keep the soil contained. I typically use a wood that doesn't break down, like cedar or redwood. Similar to the midden mound, which we'll discuss in the next chapter, I use the raised frame for composting.

People all around the world have utilized raised-bed mound gardening. The Romans utilized some of the earliest known raised bed–like mounds in home gardens by encasing their garden in submerged slate slabs or brick. They used tiles to form a type of partially submerged basin. This would form a raised bed and prevent rapid water loss due to the buried stone bottom.[58]

Wider raised-bed mounds are more beneficial when depending on rainfall as your predominant water source. The quick two-minute soil-bag mound method in the first chapter would be considered a framed raised bed, with the plastic bag itself being the soil containment frame.

Benefits:

→ This type of mound garden can provide a larger garden area in a single mound.

→ If you desire longer gardens, this would be the easiest mound type to build.

→ The raised-bed mound can catch more rainfall than the other mound types.

→ This is the most familiar type of raised mound structure.

Specifications:

→ Mound Height: Typically four to 16 inches.

→ Mound Width: Typically three to four feet.

→ Mound Length: Any length is allowed.

→ Mound Orientation: East to west (if crops are not the same height).

The Process:

1. Choose a proper location for the garden.

2. If you plan on using a framed bed, build or purchase the frame and place it in the garden location.

3. After building the framed bed, fill it with purchased or known rich local soil.

4. If building an unframed bed, shape the bed by using a garden rake to pull soil onto the newly forming bed.

5. Mix any additional soil amendments gently into the top few inches.

6. Level out the mound.

7. Add stone or framing to benefit the mounds in hot, sunny locations, as it reduces evaporation via the sides of the mounds.

For Best Results:

→ Plant non-intensively if you're going to rely on mostly rainfall for watering your crops. Utilize ollas or a drip system if you will be planting intensively.

→ Framing can hide insects or slugs, so unframed mound gardens might be more advisable if you are concerned about giving pests a place to hide.

THE NATIVE AMERICAN WAY

Amaranth grain can withstand the rigors of climate change. Amaranth is quite easy to grow. It is an adaptable plant that is full of protein, vitamins, and minerals.

Source: Fikadu Reta Alemayehu et al, "The Potential for Utilizing the Seed Crop Amaranth in East Africa as an Alternative Crop to Support Food Security and Climate Change Mitigation," *Journal of Agronomy and Crop Science* 201, no. 5 (November 2014), https://doi.org/10.1111/jac.12108

CHAPTER 12

MIDDEN MOUND GARDENS

*"The Ancient Egyptians prescribed walking through
a garden as a cure for the mad."*
—Paul Fleischman[59]

E very year I grow some of my pumpkins and tomatoes in my
midden mound garden because I know they love it. They are
probably some of the first crops that were domesticated, because
they were found to be able grow in this type of mound. I have a midden mound and scatter my waste on it, along with tea bags and coffee
grounds. I'll make a layer of coffee grounds and yard leaves. This mound
is my go-to method for getting rid of my yard waste and utilizing coffee
grounds and compostable materials.

MIDDEN MOUND BUILT ON TOP OF COMPOST PIT

If you followed the instructions to make one of the various composting piles described in Chapter 4, you are halfway to creating a midden mound garden. It's that simple. Similar to the Hügelkultur mound, midden mounds can be built by piling all of your kitchen and yard wastes into slightly raised hills and planting directly on top. You can spread out the finished compost or incorporate it into the topsoil as the ancients did over 4,000 years ago. It is speculated that the first garden crops were plants that grew tenaciously in midden mounds as far back as 10,000 years ago.[60]

You might have several composting piles throughout your garden over time. Some crops can be planted directly into your compost pile, while other crops that require a higher water intake prefer more soil. Some crops grow better in compost heaps, and others prefer a sandy or mineral-rich soil. Before you dive in and begin planting, there are a few important details to consider.

→ Thin soil layers strategically placed between the added material layers can benefit plant growth.

→ Don't put the waste of specific crops that you plan to plant in the mound due to possible disease issues. For example, tomato plant wastes should not be placed in mounds that will grow crops from the tomato family.

→ Before you plant, cover the compost mound with three inches of rich, ready-to-plant soil.

→ Periodically adding fertilizer is highly recommended.

→ The moisture content of this mound type should be monitored much more closely.

→ Certain materials, like raw manure, should not be added due to risk of potential pathogens.

→ Don't put your compost piles just anywhere. Strategic sunny locations are critical to the success of your midden mound.

Specifications:

→ Mound Height: Typically, eight to 16 inches.

→ Mound Width: Typically, 24 to 48 inches.

→ Mound Length: Any length is allowed.

→ Mound Orientation: East to west (if crops are not the same height).

The Process:

1. Choose a proper location for the garden.

2. Loosen down at least six inches into the ground soil where your mounds will be placed.

3. Place a circle—three feet in diameter and four inches high—of coffee grounds and filters, compostable paper tea bags, fresh untreated grass clippings, vegetable/fruit scraps, chopped fresh nonflowering weeds, or quality compost on the mound location. Moisten this layer.

4. Add two inches of rich soil.

5. Cover this material with a six-inch layer of dried shredded leaves, dried untreated straw (not hay), dried non seeding weeds or grass clippings, shredded dried corn stalks.

6. Cover this material with a three-inch layer of rich soil.

7. Lay down a one-inch layer of mulch.

8. Keep the mound moist to encourage decomposition of the core material.

For Best Results:

→ Choose crops that are known to be good compost pile growers.

→ Occasionally use organic liquid fertilizers such as fish emulsion or seaweed extracts to give the compost mound a little boost of essential minerals not commonly found in compost.

→ Make it a goal to continuously build the mound with soil or completed compost.

→ You may have issues growing some root crops due to soil level drops when the compost decomposes.

→ Just like with the Hügelkultur mound, it's best to build compost mounds months in advance.

→ Keep your midden mound moist, but not sopping wet.

→ If not planted yet, cover it with a tarp if it is already moist throughout and you suspect a long-duration rain event.

→ Your mound should start to smell earthy and woodsy, not swampy or sour.

→ It will also attain a brown to black color and become crumbly to the touch.

→ Remember that smaller pieces of anything you add will decay faster.

→ Try freezing any material that comes from your kitchen. The material will turn a little mushy and decay much faster, as the cell walls will burst when the materials are frozen.

I noticed that my midden mounds became dryer and slower at decomposing when I didn't have plants in them, due to the fact that I didn't visit them when I wasn't adding compost materials. (I automatically brought my hose or watering bucket up to my midden mounds when I started growing pumpkins in them.) This type of mound will shrink faster than any of the other mound types due to the higher content of organic material. This is why it's good to keep adding compost and a layer of mulch to the top.

Now that you're familiar with all of the popular mound garden methods, you can also experiment with added features. You can choose to mix and match features from different methods to enhance the building of the soil and the health of the crops being grown. In the next chapter, you will find tips on mound maintenance.

CHAPTER 13

BEYOND WEEDING: 10 MORE TECHNIQUES TO MAXIMIZE ABUNDANCE

"It is the year which bears, and not the field."
—Ancient Greek proverb[61]

N**ow that you** have your perfect mound garden built and planted, it's time to nurture it. No matter how large or small your garden may be, your new goal is to maintain constant growth. Providing consistent water, sunlight, nutrients, and protection from pests, weather, and disease will help your crops thrive, so they can provide you a bountiful harvest. Keeping weeds at bay with mulch and reliable watering with ollas every couple of days will make the process much easier and rewarding in the long run.

You might do everything right only for some unknown variable to come into play. A freak frost, a new plant disease, or a hoard of ravenous moose could ruin your crop. Don't let that scare you away from planting your mound garden. The best way to compensate for those unknown variables and potential losses is to plant a little more than you initially thought you should. That will tip the odds of succeeding in your favor.

At the end of the day, it will come down to you. I've discovered that maintaining your garden becomes even easier if it's right outside your door or near your driveway. There is some truth to the adage "out of sight, out of mind." You can gauge your level of obsession by the number of times you check on your garden in a single day. As with caring for children, the more you check on your gardens, the better. Let's get specific and break down the maintenance.

Weeding

Weeds are detrimental to crops because they steal nutrients, water, and valuable garden space. However, weeds should not be an issue if you mulch your garden and completely pull up the few weeds that may pop up in your soft, friable soil. Weeds are typically a nuisance the first month after sowing seed or transplanting starts. The smaller surface areas of your mound garden should make weeding a simple chore should the need arise. You can use a weeding hoe on the open areas between the mounds, but it is best to handpick the weeds on the mounds themselves. It can be a tedious task but be proactive and pull out weeds as you see them; otherwise, they will just get worse.

Here are a few tips to prevent weeds in your garden:

→ Mulch your mounds and the spaces in between them.

→ Utilize polyculture, intensive planting, or cover crops to crowd out the weeds.

→ Make sure you pull weeds out roots and all.

→ Intensively plant if you will be the main source of water for your crops. This will also shade out any sprouting weeds.

→ Use an olla, which will water the soil beneath the surface and keep the upper soil areas dryer, thus inhibiting weed germination.

→ Do not use herbicides, as they are bad for your soil, your crops, and you. Using organic corn gluten meal (with 60 percent protein) in the spring can be a good alternative.

Weeds are the main reason why I turned away from conventional gardening. When I first moved to Virginia in 2001, I tried gardening the conventional way. I dug up a big area and planted in rows, but it would just sprout weeds. If I didn't go out there for a few days after the rain, weeds were everywhere. The plants would grow together, and the weeds would grow in between. I took up mound gardening because the smaller plots and loose soil made weeding almost a non-issue. And when weeds do grow in your mound garden, you can spot them and easily remove them.

Watering

If your garden was not designed to utilize only rainfall, you will need to either use a device or do the watering yourself. Proper watering is critical because of these issues:

→ Too little water can cause dry-pot setback, which is when the delicate root hairs die and the plant is thrown off the constant growth phase.

→ Too much water prevents oxygen from getting to the roots, thus causing stress and probably rot as the plants start to die.

It's best to water your crops when the soil about an inch or two below the surface feels dry to the touch. Also, don't forget to rid your garden of weeds, because they can rob your crops of water.

Overall, your garden should receive about an inch or two of water or rainfall per week to ensure healthy growth. Your soil type and soil additions can go a long way in alleviating your need to water your crops. A rich and healthy soil that is abundant in organic matter and soil life, with a top covering of soil-building mulch, can mean the difference between watering every day or every few days.

CONDUCT A SOIL MOISTURE TEST

Stick your finger into the soil near the base of your plant. Make sure to go down to about your second knuckle. If your finger comes out relatively clean, then that area requires watering. If your finger comes out smeared with soil, then there should be enough moisture in the soil.

When I had my conventional garden, there were times when, after days of heavy rains, my yellow squash and zucchini had rotted. I had used my local soil, which was a clay soil, without mixture or compost, and the crops couldn't handle the excess water. That has never happened with any of my mound gardens. It could rain for days, and because the mounds are raised, high in organic matter, and free draining, they don't experience the same problem. The plants love it!

Here are some tips to ensure the proper watering of your mound garden.

→ Watering deeply and less often will help develop deep roots and condition the plants to not require constant watering. As a guideline, you should water down to about eight inches or more, and then let the top two inches dry before you water deeply again.

→ Water in the morning, as this will allow more water to get to the roots due to less evaporation. Only water in the evening if you absolutely have to.

→ Apply water at the base of the plant. Do not water the leaves as this can promote fungus growth and disease.

→ Utilize ollas to get the water below the soil surface where it is needed.

→ Water the entire grow area, because the dry, non-watered areas will absorb water away from your crops.

→ Keep a thin layer of mulch on your mounds so that water can penetrate it and go deep into your soil. If the mulch layer is too thick or too fine, it will prevent water from filtering down. Roughen up the soil surface with a rake if you don't have mulch, as this will also allow water to penetrate a tough crusty soil surface. Over time, these soil crusts will develop on un-mulched garden soil.

→ Create a central mound low point so that water will concentrate and penetrate deeply into the mound.

Avoiding Soil Compaction

Precious air and water are unable to filter down deep into compacted soil, so it is important not to walk or tamp on the mounds in your garden, especially if the ground is very wet. This negatively affects the health of plant roots, which require soil oxygen and water for proper growth.

Compacted soil also inhibits root growth due to the physical restrictions of the dense soil.

The best way to test for soil compaction is with a long metal rod or rebar. The rod should move down through soil when you apply steady and even pressure. You can also perform the ribbon or ball soil test from Chapter 3. Compaction will naturally occur if the soil is high in clay.

Here are some more tips to avoid soil compaction:

→ Ensure that the soil in your garden mounds is rich in loose organic materials and not predominantly clay.

→ Do not excessively tamp or walk on the mounds you build.

→ Use planks placed around the mounds if attempting not to impact the soil in between them.

→ Ensure proper mound spacing and size so that there will be no need to walk on them.

→ Perform periodic soil compaction tests in the early spring before you plant. Your plants will thank you with abundant growth.

Soil Building

It's important to keep your soil healthy, friable, and nutrient rich, as this will keep your crops and soil well-nourished and thriving. This constant soil building, and the avoidance of tilling, will prevent the rapid oxidation of the soil's organic matter and the loss of any new topsoil that you create. The topsoil region is the most critical zone for crop growth.

Keeping the soil moist and rich with organic matter allows the soil microbes to thrive and perform their critical task of decomposition, thus producing nutrients for your crops. Utilizing cover crops that are strong partners with mycorrhizae will ensure that a healthy population of the fungi is present in your mounds, thus helping to contribute to your soil building nutrients and soil organisms. A healthy mix of fungi, bacteria, and other soil organisms will assist in healthy plant growth.

Use these ideas to continually build and enhance your soil:

→ At the end of your growing season, cover the tops of your mounds with about three inches of rich, quality chunky compost. You can then plant cover crops or mulch to protect the mound from erosion.

→ Occasional additions of worm castings, compost tea, or organic fertilizers will also enhance the soil.

→ Mulching with pure compost combines the benefits of mulching and soil building.

💡 EXPERT TIP

Continually monitor for issues. Manually check for pests and diseases and utilize prevention techniques and organic methods to control them. Try to do a quick daily inspection if possible. The sooner you detect an issue, the easier it will be to resolve it.

Mulching

Any kind of material that's placed on top of your soil (organic or nonorganic) is considered mulch. Mulching will save you time when watering, weeding, fertilizing, or hauling away your grass clippings or leaves. It can also add beauty to your garden while giving you easier access to your plants, especially the lower parts for harvesting or cleaning due to the lack of weeds around the base of your crops. It also allows you to walk unimpeded between your mounds and without stepping through weeds. Basically, it would be a mistake not to utilize mulching. Just make sure that you don't mulch up the stem of your crops, because this can cause rot and pest issues.

You'll typically need a mulch layer of about one to two inches. It would also be wise to mulch the areas between your mounds and in adjacent future mound locations to keep weeds and other pests at bay. A three- to four-inch layer of mulch would be more ideal, as it would prevent bare spots from occurring due to the thicker layer. Try to utilize free sources of mulch, such as untreated grass clippings or leaves, because you will use a lot of it.

EXPERT TIP

You'll need to make sure your soil is warm and moist before laying down a thick insulating layer of mulch. Laying mulch on top of cold dry soil will only curtail any plant growth. Another free and beneficial way to mulch is to utilize intensive planting, which will shade and effectively perform a mulching function without using a physical mulch material.

The benefits of mulching include the following:

→ Prevents weeds.

→ Moderates soil temperatures in both summer and winter.

→ Slows evaporation.

→ Prevents soil erosion and soil-nutrient loss.

→ Fertilizes your soil and crops, since mulching is a basic form of sheet composting.

→ Prevents soil splash, which can transfer disease organisms to the plant leaves.

→ Prevents soil crusting, which can cause increased water runoff and slow water absorption.

Common mulch materials can include these elements:

→ Shredded leaves.

→ Untreated dried grass clipping.

→ Compost.

→ Non-treated straw.

→ Shredded bark mulch.

→ Leaf mold.

→ Gravel.

→ Landscape fabric.

Continual Harvesting

Continual harvesting is the method of consistently picking your crops so that the plant continues to produce over the entire growing season. This can be effective with crops like Seminole pumpkins, zucchini, squash, and especially cucumbers.

You'll want to pick a crop like cucumbers frequently, because if you leave one cucumber growing on the vine, the production of the whole plant will gradually slow down. The job of the plant is to produce seeds for the next generation, and once it's made a fruit that is fully ripe, the plant believes that its job is done. However, if you keep picking the crop continuously, you basically fool the plant into thinking that it hasn't accomplished its goal. Not only will harvesting improve yields, but some plants will stop producing fruit if they are not harvested at the proper time.

Make sure you don't damage your plants during harvesting. Use scissors or a knife to cut the stem of the fruit, thus eliminating damage to the plant's stems and branches. The ancient Romans and Native American tribes of the past agreed that harvesting is best done before the sun makes the late morning too hot.[62]

Pruning, Pinching, Thinning, and Cleaning

Some basic ritual cleanup work in your garden will go a long way in keeping your crops healthy. The pruning, pinching, and cleaning will aid in airflow throughout your garden, thus helping prevent possible fungal infections, pest infestations, and other diseases. Some Native American tribes performed post-garden season cleanup in the spring, just before planting. The residual crop materials would be burned in the garden because they preferred for their gardens to be clean and weed-free.[63]

Fertilizing

An ancient Greek saying states that you should never put your crops in soil that is less healthy and nutrient rich than the soil in which the seeds were started.[64] One important goal is to start your garden with nutrient-rich soil.

There is no question that fertilizing will benefit your crops, but don't overdo it. Over-fertilizing, especially with nitrogen, not only makes your crops more attractive to pests, but it could also reduce your harvestable bounty since it will produce more leaf and branch materials on the plants. It is very important to follow the directions on the fertilizer package.

Try to use an organic fertilizer because it will benefit your soil in the long term. Remember to feed the soil, not the plant. If you correctly feed and take care of the soil, the soil will take care of your plants.

Luckily, the mound garden structure increases the speed and efficiency of the decomposition of reintroduced decomposable plant materials and organic fertilizers.

Reapply fertilizers after any prolonged rain events. These periodic dressings of compost or worm castings under your mulch layer will greatly enhance crop growth and increase the critical organic matter levels of your mound.

Here are some common fertilizer choices:

→ *Compost teas:* These solutions can be diluted and sprayed on the leaves to feed the crops and prevent some leaf diseases. They can also be poured into the soil around the root area.

→ *Plant extract teas (comfrey tea, dandelion tea):* These teas are made the same way as compost tea, but using fresh, un-composted plant materials. There are numerous plants that can be used, but a few especially provide a fertilizing punch to mound gardens.

→ *Worm castings:* These are essentially worm digestion byproducts (aka worm excrement). They are not only nutrient rich, but they also have soil-conditioning attributes that will benefit your crops and the health of the soil.

→ *Cover crops:* These are specific plants that are usually sown on a garden location after the main crop has been harvested. These plants are typically in the legume family due to their increased nitrogen-fixing capabilities and nutrient content. Just before the next vegetable crop is sown in a location, cut down the cover crop in place and mix it into the soil. This releases all the stored nutrients when decomposition starts on the recently cut-down cover crops. Typical cover crops include red clover, hairy vetch, and mustard.

→ *Commercial organic liquid and dry fertilizers:* Using organic fertilizers as instructed will usually translate into healthy crop growth. Organic fertilizers usually decompose at a slow rate, thus spreading out nutrient availability and preventing nutrient burn. You'll need to follow the directions, but slight overdoses won't usually cause any harm due to the slower spread of the nutrients.

→ *Commercial nonorganic liquid and dry fertilizers (use only in emergencies):* Chemical fertilizers fit into this category. The use of this type of fertilizer is beneficial at first, but salt will begin to build up and can harm the soil with continued use.

These tips can help with fertilizing:

→ Always follow the directions on purchased fertilizers.

→ In general, never feed during plant dormancy, flowering, or heat waves.

→ Keeping the soil covered with mulch will protect the rapid degradation of any fertilizer or compost applied to the top of your soil.

→ Keeping the soil consistently moist will maintain constant soil microbe activity, thus a steady nutrient supply.

→ Stick with organic fertilizers, as nonorganic fertilizers will build up and eventually harm the soil.

→ Make your own free nutrients by utilizing compost piles, compost teas, cover crops, and plant-based teas.

Providing Plant Supports

Ideally you want your crops to grow up, not across, your garden. Some crops, such as cucumbers and pumpkins, have a better shape and are less prone to surface blemishes or rot when sitting on the ground due to their fruit. Those crops aside, growing up increases vital air circulation throughout your garden, thus decreasing the risk of fungal and other diseases. Some crops need support, as their heavy fruiting can cause their branches to break. Here are two methods for supporting your plants:

→ Staking: This is the process of attaching tall plants to a pole or cage to prevent them from falling over and resting on the ground. This will ensure healthy airflow between the plants, thus reducing mildews, molds, and fungal infections. The crop will also be protected from ground-crawling creatures and moisture damage.

→ Trellising: Similar to using a pole or cage for staking, trellising utilizes a trellis, which is a ladder-like device offering more attachment points for one plant or providing multiple plants a location to be staked without growing on top of each other. This process can work as a decoration, too.

Dealing with Pests

Prevention and control should be your focus when dealing with pests in your mound garden. Daily inspections and hand removal of pests should be a priority. Look for signs of insects and their eggs and remove them by hand. Everything is connected, and keeping your soil and plants healthy, while not overfertilizing with nitrogen, will go a long way in preventing pests and diseases. Watering properly and keeping the garden tidy will also strengthen the plants in your mound garden and prevent pests.

Vine borers are the reason I gravitated toward the Seminole pumpkin. When trying to grow pumpkin, squash, and cucumber, so many gardeners encounter problems with vine borers. This is a moth that lays an egg at the base of the vine where the vine meets the soil. A grub then grows inside and eats the vine. The borer cuts off all the water and nutrients, so the vine essentially turns to mush and kills the plant. This is a chronic problem for pumpkin and squash. In my gardens, sometimes two out of five of these plants will succumb to vine borers. However, the vine of the Seminole pumpkin is so hard that it's immune to vine borers.

Certain plants and vegetables create defenses within themselves (chemicals and smells) that are used as deterrents against pests. Marigolds and garlic are good examples. A well-planned garden will have these plants mixed in with other crops to serve as pest deterrents. The seeds from these manmade crops and hybrids are especially prized if they produce crops that are tasty and nutritious, too. Seed catalogs will often provide a code at the bottom of the plant description that describes to which diseases it is resistant. Most vegetables have varieties that offer more disease resistance than others.

Keep in mind that if the plot is overplanted, certain insects can travel across the entire garden just by crawling from one plant to the next. Sporadic spacing of plants will confuse insects and prevent easy access to the crop they want. Barriers between small groupings of plants can help guard against further infestation.

Other plants need sufficient spacing between them to prevent the pests and diseases to which they might be susceptible. For example, tomato plants become susceptible to fungal infections if they don't have enough airflow. Proper spacing allows the leaves to dry faster after rain or a heavy morning dew, preventing the moist and stagnant environment where fungi and diseases thrive. The goal is to make things difficult for insects and prevent other maladies that can ruin your crop.

You can also try these pest-prevention ideas:

→ Early intervention and preventative tactics will go a long way in making your garden disease- and pest-free, but you'll never be totally pest-free. Growing extra crops will allow you to still get a great harvest even after unavoidable losses due to Mother Nature's other creations.

→ Use a spray bottle of water to blast away aphids to prevent a larger infestation.

→ Use row covers during the main growth phase and remove for a few hours at a time when crops are flowering and need bees to fertilize the flowers.

→ Sprinkle crushed eggshells, red or black pepper mixtures, or coffee grounds on the soil around your plants to help repel slugs and other pests.

→ Make garlic and cayenne pepper sprays to use on the tops and bottoms of leaves. Spray daily if needed.

→ A compost tea sprayed on top and beneath the leaves every two weeks will inhibit the growth of some fungi. Foliar feeding with compost tea will not only boost crop growth but may also protect your plants from diseases.

→ Protect from vine borers and cut worms by using collars of tin foil at the stem or soil line of your plants, especially with squash, pumpkin, and bean plants.

→ Consider utilizing beneficial insects such as ladybugs, praying mantis, and parasitic wasps.

→ Grow disease- and pest-resistant varieties of crops.

Not all pests are the same, so you'll need to use different techniques when removing certain pests from your garden. Two of the most pervasive pests are worms and aphids.

Every year, no matter what season I grow, I will find small worm eggs under the leaves of my cabbage where they try to hide. They are orange, like the size of a large pinhead. Because they are almost glued on there, you must scrape them off, so you don't get a brood of worms. This is why you need to use row covers over your cabbage. If you don't, you're going to get worms, and those worms are voracious. If you let them get big, they could eat your entire plant, so if you catch them early you will save yourself a lot of crop loss.

You'll want to take this same approach for tomatoes, but you'll be looking for a big, green tomato worm instead. Be sure to pick them off when they're small, because once they hatch and disperse, they are green and therefore hard to see. They, too, can do a lot of damage. I make it a goal to search for these worms every year, but I always seem to rush and miss that one plant that ends up suffering as a result.

Aphids are small, sap-sucking insects that are about the size of a pinhead, but they reproduce exponentially, so one can turn into 20 in a single day. They suck the juice out of the leaves, which then turn yellow and blotchy. You want to be proactive with aphids and can spray them off your crops with a hose. You don't need chemicals because they are small, so gently spraying your leaves is enough to knock them off.

Being proactive early on with crop inspections can go a long way to prevent pest and fungal infestations. Pests can double overnight, so be careful. My go-to methods are row covers (plant netting) or BT spray. BT is a natural, non-pathogenic bacterium that is toxic only to worms. Netting will prevent the egg-laying insects access to your crops, but for the plants that require pollination, such as tomatoes, the netting will need to be removed at times to allow bees and other pollinators to go in and fertilize the flowers that will ultimately turn into fruit.

PROTECTING YOUR MOUND GARDEN FROM THE WEATHER

Use shade cloth or shade structures to protect your crops from the intense, hot summer sun. Use walls, berms, and tall growth to protect your crops from strong winds. Make sure your garden mounds are constructed on the sides of a gentle southern slope.

Growth-Enhancing and Propagation Techniques

Plant propagation is the process of growing new plants from cuttings of existing plants. The ancient Greeks and Romans used propagation as a speedy and efficient way to replicate their prized crops, especially hardy and bountiful individual plants. For example, picture a herder breeding his prized bull. Consider propagation the same as making clones of your strongest plants.[65] Think back to the vine borer example. Maybe those three yellow squash plants that survived the vine borer had something in their DNA that made them more resilient than the other two that died. So, why not take cuttings from those surviving plants, soak them in water so they sprout roots, and then plant them? Plant propagation provides a great way to get extra versions of your heartiest plants without having to wait for them to sprout and grow like you would if planting a seed. The stem you cut from the existing plant could be eight months old, so as soon as you bury it in the soil, it's ready to start producing vegetables. This method also works very well with strawberries.

When wine was popular with the Romans thousands of years ago, they mastered numerous propagation techniques for their vineyards. Quintilianus, a second-century Roman educator, said:

"So that vines will bear fruit to their capacity, it is necessary to note those that bear a good crop or a heavy crop, may have buds, and are unblemished; mark these and at planting time, take new plants from them; not from vines that are themselves newly planted, because they are too weak, not from ageing ones, because they are barren, but from vines in their first flourishing or a little further advanced."[66]

There are many things you can do to enhance the growth of your crops. One example would be to allow portions of your pumpkin vines to root into rich soil, thus increasing the amount of nutrients available. This often translates into a healthier plant and a larger crop yield. Strawberry runners can be allowed to root, thus increasing the number of plants you have. Also, take cuttings of your plants that are known to be good candidates for propagation. Using this method, you should plant more of these plants, as the wildlife will try to get their fill of your crops. A lot of this comes down to trial and error, but with some crops you can tell just by looking at them if they have primordial roots growing. For example, some crops have leaf or branch extensions that have primordial root-like structures growing off of them that appear as though they can be cut off and would root easily.

THE NATIVE AMERICAN WAY

Native American tribes of the past were known to plant morning glories near their melon seeds, because the morning glories exuded growth stimulants, thus speeding up seed germination.

CHAPTER 14

THE FOUR R'S TO A YEAR-LONG HARVEST: REAP AND REPEAT, ROTATE, AND REBUILD

"If we take care of the seeds, they will take care of us."
—Native American proverb[67]

Harvesting your crops should be a time of jubilation. You might not host a neighborhood harvest festival but celebrate the harvest nonetheless, because you deserve it!

I hope that you took some notes along the way. Some crops will require constant harvesting, such as tomatoes and cucumbers, so make sure you harvest these crops as soon as they ripen. It might be crucial, as some plants will stop producing if they sense fully ripe fruit still hanging on their branches. Other crops will be harvested all at once, such as corn, unless you spaced out the planting in batches.

Crop Rotation

Try not to plant crops from the same family in the newly available mound. Crop rotation will ensure that garden pests and nutrient depletion will be minimized, because a different crop usually means that a different set of pests and nutrient requirements will come into play. If you plant the same crops over and over, then a specific garden pest may take up permanent residence. Planting the same crops will also continue to deplete the same nutrients from the mound, thus causing a deficiency.

Post-Harvest Soil Building

Your main goal post-harvest is to maintain soil quality and health. You'll want to keep your soil loose and friable by topping it off with a two- to three-inch layer of compost and then planting a cover crop such as daikon radishes or snap peas to till your soil down deep. The additional benefit of these cover crops is that they are edible.

A good plan for post-harvest would be to do what Native American tribes did on planting day, utilizing a couple of modern permaculture techniques to enhance the process.[68]

→ Remove dead roots and other plant wastes and put them in your compost pit.

→ Gently loosen the soil with a digging stick or hoe.

→ Lay down two to three inches of compost and cover with a thin layer of mulch or a cover crop.

DID YOU KNOW?

Native peoples of British Colombia used permaculture techniques to raise and harvest the same perennial plants year after year.

Source: Tenenbaum, "Farming, Native American Style."

Three-Season Mound Gardening

When you start harvesting your warm-season crops, it might be time to think about planting your cool-season crops in the newly freed-up space. To maximize your gardening fun and yield, you should be able to get in multiple planting sessions (about three) within a single year. These sessions include spring crops (cool-season crops), summer crops (warm-season crops), and fall crops (another cool-season garden).

You can plant cool season crops on your mounds as soon as the soil is workable. Crops such as peas, lettuces, spinach, and other greens can be planted on your mound edges and centers in early spring. When May rolls around and warm-season crops can be planted, you can harvest the center areas to make room for your corn or tomatoes. Just remember to add another dose of quality compost to the center of the mound before you plant your warm-season crops. You can continue planting the cool-season crops on the edges and on the northern side of your warm-season crops, and they should stay cooler due to the shading provided by the summer crops. You can then start planting cool season crops again in mid to late summer on the southern edges of the mounds.

Depending on your growing site and growing techniques, you may be able to keep some of the following super hardy crops alive throughout the entire winter:

→   Carrots.

→ Cabbage.

→ Spinach.

→ Collards.

→ Kale.

→ Swiss Chard.

The frost increases the sugar content of these crops, which not only protects them from bitter cold, but also sweetens their flavors. Ultimately, I recommend that you try to keep something growing in your mounds year-round. What do you have to lose?

One of the difficulties of gardening during the winter months is that the sun is not as strong. Warmth can help the plants grow a little faster, but it's really the strength of the sun that fuels growth. I'll grow cabbage and kale; even though I don't get much from the crop (maybe a couple bowls of leaves every three weeks), the goal is to keep gardening.

The Impact of Climate Change

In the winter of 2019–2020, most of my outdoor-planted cool season crops survived. I didn't even need to bring in the potted plants I have on my deck. I had started planting in pots because I could always pull them off the deck and bring them inside if I knew a hard frost was coming and that the plants might not make it. I didn't have to do that the past few years, and the plants in pots would die sooner than the plants in mounds. So, if the plants in pots were surviving, the mounds had no way of dying, and my mounds have recently been producing almost year-round. Three or four years earlier, my cabbage would barely grow, and now I'm harvesting more. Not only are the plants surviving, but so are some of the insects, which means that pests come out earlier to lay their eggs.

Why is this happening? The sun isn't stronger. The light isn't changing. We're still the same distance from the sun. The only thing that has changed is the climate. The impact of the changing climate will only continue to impact gardening and crop growth. For example, more rain events could naturally translate to more fungal and mildew infestations. There are even some predictions that say that crops might become less nutritious.[69] It's difficult to predict all of the changes we might face, but one thing is for certain—if we continue to go down this road, it will only make conditions worse for our crops.

CHAPTER 15

GARDENING BY THE MOON

"Every little thing is sent for something, and in that thing, there should be happiness and the power to make happy. Like the grasses showing tender faces to each other, this we should do."
—Black Elk, Oglala Lakota Native, American Medicine Man[70]

A s the ancient Roman astronomer named Ptolemy once stated, "The sun by the dryness of its own fire draws out the moist element. Conversely the moon is in itself moistening, effecting mixture and dilution."[71]

It is well known that the moon has great influence on both humans and the earth. Life on Earth and the physical world as we know it would not be the same if the moon had never existed. Natural Earth cycles, such as the tides, use the moon as their clock, giving us proof of its power and influence.

Many ancient cultures believed that the moon had a positive impact on their crops. The coming and going of the moons were reminders of the seasons for many ancient gardeners. It stands to reason that the ancients gardened by the moon phases and have passed that wisdom on to modern gardeners.[72]

The many gardening tasks that can be guided by the moon phases include planting, harvesting, grafting, weeding, and preserving. You, too, can embrace this ancient knowledge and learn the effects of the moon on your mound garden. Start by familiarizing yourself with the following terms:

→ *Waxing moon:* The phase when the moon grows larger each night and increases in illumination.

→ *Waning moon:* The phase when the moon becomes smaller each night and decreases in illumination.

→ *New moon:* When there is no moon present in the night sky.

→ *Full moon:* When the moon is fully illuminated. Of course, we never see the dark side of the moon.[73]

♀ EXPERT TIP

During the waxing moon, when the moonlight is on the right, plant your tomatoes in full sight (moving from new moon to full, planting is best when the moon is in its first quarter). During the waning moon, when the moonlight is on the left, planting potatoes would be best (moving from full moon to new). Planting crops with aboveground fruits is said to benefit from the extra gravity pull of a waxing moon. Water is pulled up into the stems and leaves. Root crops are traditionally best planted on a waning moon, when the water pulled up into the plant is less.

WHEN TO MOON GARDEN

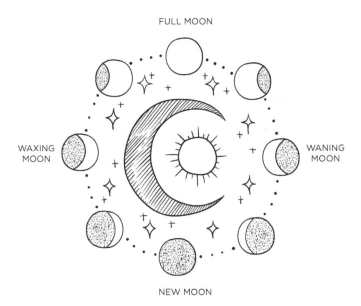

FULL MOON

WAXING MOON

WANING MOON

NEW MOON

Ancient Roman gardening manuals advised that nothing should be planted when the moon is waning, and everything should be planted on the waxing moon.[74] Planting on the waxing moon will hasten germination and promote more rapid growth due to the moon's gravity increasing the water content of the upper soil regions and the water flow through the leaves.[75]

Weeding is likely best done on a waxing moon, as more weed seeds should germinate due to the increased upper soil moisture content. It is also beneficial to plant the seeds and have the plants sprout in increasing moonlight, as nocturnal crop predators will be less apt to move about in the bright of the moon.

You can also use the moon phases to guide you in doing these other garden tasks:

→ *Grafting:* Perform this task on a waxing moon when healing fluids would be drawn up towards the graft area.[76]

→ *Weeding:* Start pulling weeds upon the new moon on into the full moon.

→ *Harvesting:* Harvest your crops on the new moon to give them a longer shelf life.

Native American Full Moon Names by Month

Native American tribes developed a novel way of tracking seasons and their gardening periods by naming each month's full moon. They would also call each month by these same names. Legends, lore, and oral traditions were tied to these names, and these stories were often told during the long, cold nights of winter when the harvest was long over and the cold weather limited outdoor activities to hunting and wood gathering.[77]

These names may differ depending on the tribe and their location, but here is a list of commonly used moon names.[78]

→ January/Wolf Moon: The howling of hungry wolves searching for food in the very cold air inspired this name.

→ February/Snow Moon: This month's full moon name was derived from the large amounts of snowfall during this time of the year.

→ March/Worm Moon: The observation of increased earthworm activity following the cold winter, thus signaling the upcoming crop-growing season, gives this month its full moon name.

→ April/Flower Moon: The first appearance of the wildflower blooms normally occurs this time of year, thus the name of the month.

→ May/Corn Planting Moon: Warming soil signaled the need to plant corn during this month.

→ June/Strawberry Moon: The ripening of many strawberries this time of year influenced the name of this month's full moon.

→ July/Buck Moon: This month's full moon name was derived from the observation of male deer rubbing the velvet off of their newly formed antlers.

→ August/Corn Moon: The ripening and harvesting of corn starts during this month.

→ September/Harvest Moon: The ripening and harvesting of the major crops (corn, squash, and beans) occur during this month, thus inspiring the name.

→ October/Hunter's Moon: This month's full moon name was derived from the observation that game animals were starting to fatten up for the long cold winter.

→ November/Frost Moon: Frosts typically start during this month.

→ December/Cold Moon: The bitter cold of winter aptly helped inspire the name of this month's full moon.

Your task this month is to learn the full moon name and to venture outside to view the moon. Give a simple thank you to our heavenly master and the ancients who paved the way for some of the gardening techniques provided in this book.

THE NATIVE AMERICAN WAY

There were quite a few Native American tribes that performed their planting on the waxing moon, as they believed that the seeds and sprouts extracted the strength of the brightening moon to help them grow.

GARDENING BY THE STARS

Generations long ago also utilized the stars or zodiac to govern their planting schedules. More so than the moon, stars and constellations require much darker and clearer skies to be effectively seen. These are two of the most notable gardening signs provided by our cosmos:

1. When Arcturus (fourth brightest star in the sky) rises high and traverses the entire sky, spring is right around the corner. Arcturus resides in the constellation Scorpio.

2. When Orion makes its presence known by rising in the east just after sunset, you know winter is just around the corner and it's time to harvest.[79]

PHENOLOGY

Phenology is the practice of using biological occurrences in nature as a timing guide to planting crops or expecting pest emergence. This science goes back to antiquity, with the oldest documentation being 974 BC.[80][81]

It is said that Native American women would often look for these natural signs (such as leaf growth on specific plants or trees, flower buds opening, or animal migrations) when they were out in the woods foraging for food before the planting season.[82] Many cultures have utilized phenological observations to some degree, with modern science taking special interest in lilac and saucer magnolia as common indicator plants.[83]

To become more proficient in phenology, try making your own log of these natural cycles, such as bloom times and insect emergences. You can then correlate them with your planting schedules. Better yet, you can grow some indicator plants, which will make your learning quicker.

My goal is to have as many types of indicator plants as possible to determine which ones are the most reliable. I have the following indicator plants:

→ Forsythia: This was already present in my yard when I bought the house.

→ Lilacs: These bushes were purchases before I even knew anything about phenology. My wife wanted lilac bushes because of the beautiful strong-scented flowers. Now I have four giant bushes.

→ Dandelions: I now use these as indicator plants, even though I had no plans to have them in my yard. They were provided by Mother Nature free of charge.

Time will tell how climate change will impact phenology, since changes in the climate may have profound effects on plant and animal life. Who knows? Reproduction and growth cycles may go awry.

You can use this list of common indicator plants to determine the best timing for planting.

→ Plant warm season crops when the dogwood flowers appear.

→ Plant beans, squash, and cucumbers when lilacs are in full bloom.

→ Plant beets, carrots, cole crops, lettuce, and spinach when the lilacs are in first leaf.

→ Plant peas and onions when forsythia or the common chickweed blooms, but make sure the soil is not too wet and is workable.

→ Plant potatoes when the first dandelion blooms.

→ Plant onions when red maple trees bloom.

→ Plant tomatoes, eggplant, peppers, and melons when chicory is in full bloom.

→ When the first flowers of chicory open, it is time to prevent damage from the squash vine borer.

SIMPLIFIED SEASONAL CALENDAR

Use the seasons throughout the year to plan and make the most of your gardening.

Fall: Before Planting Season

1. Build new mounds in the most optimal locations or enrich existing mounds.

2. Cover existing mounds with three inches of rich compost and then cover with mulch. Alternatively, you can gently mix in any cover crops that were grown on the mound or gathered elsewhere. Ensure that this material is disease-free.

3. Make compost.

Winter: Planning Your Growing Season

1. Choose the crops that you would like to plant. Ideally you should choose rugged and trouble-free crops that are known to grow well in your area. Your local Cooperative Extension or Master Gardener group should have a list of the crops that grow very well in your specific area.

2. Plan and draw out on paper which mounds will be used for which crops. For example, put tall crops in the northern end of

your garden. Figure out the proper number of plants per mound, which will depend on the type you have built.

3. Place any trellising on the mounds that will require plant supports.

4. Continue making compost.

Spring: Planting Your Mound Garden

1. Gently loosen your mound soil (without tilling) and hoe any soil back up that has spread away from your mounds. Lay down two to three inches of quality compost if you had not done so the previous fall. Perform a soil compaction test and resolve any issues.

2. Plant your mounds.

3. Mulch your mounds only when the soil is moist and warm (above 60 degrees Fahrenheit).

4. Protect your crops from late frosts and animal or fungal pests.

5. Continue making compost.

Summer: Maintaining and Harvesting Your Mound Garden

1. Inspect the mulch cover and add or rebuild if needed.

2. Ensure proper watering.

3. Keep the garden weed-free.

4. Protect the garden from weather, animals, insects, and soil and microbial issues.

5. Feed the soil and plants with compost teas or a weak dilution of organic fertilizers, except during heat waves.

6. Continue harvesting.

7. Continue making compost.

Gardening is so much more than a calming hobby that allows me to get back in touch with nature. I've always thought of gardening as being something bigger than I am, and I want to use it to help others. Yes, my obsession with these ancient gardening techniques is a meditative and soothing way to honor the past, but I also believe that looking to the past will help us survive the future. Those cultures of the past that we've discussed utilized these mound-gardening techniques during a time when tools were limited and there were no chemical fertilizers. Yet, mound gardens can be much more productive and easier to maintain than conventional gardens.

Native American tribes of the past and the ancient Greeks and Romans were on to something. They got it right. While we live in a time when we never know when the next pandemic or natural disaster could change our lives without warning, these techniques might become more than just useful. They might become essential, not only to ensure your life and that of your family, but also for humankind.

THE END

ENDNOTES

1   Cicero, *Epistulae and Familiares* (Chicago: Perseus, 2018),
9.4., http://perseus.uchicago.edu/perseus-cgi/citequery3.
pl?dbname=PerseusLatinTexts&getid=1&query=Cic.%20Fam.%209.4.

2   Amanda J. Landon, "The 'How' of the Three Sisters: The Origins of Agriculture in
Mesoamerica and the Human Niche," *Nebraska Anthropologist* (2008): 110–124.

3   "Chinampa," Britannica, accessed January 14, 2021, https://www.britannica.com/
topic/chinampa.

4   Tejal Rao, "Food Supply Anxiety Brings Back Victory Gardens," the *New York
Times*, March 25, 2020, https://www.nytimes.com/2020/03/25/dining/victory-
gardens-coronavirus.html.

5   Anthony Johnson, *Life Begins The Day You Start A Garden: A story based in the
tradition of Chinese proverbs* (Water Bearer Herbs, 2013).

6   Zeke Hausather, "Explainer: What Climate Models Tell Us about Future Rainfall,"
Carbon Brief, January 18, 2018, https://www.carbonbrief.org/explainer-what-
climate-models-tell-us-about-future-rainfall.

7   Wendell Berry, *The Unforeseen Wilderness: An Essay on Kentucky's Red River Gorge*
(Lexington, KY: University Press of Kentucky, 1971), 26.

8 "Management of Sandy Soils," Food and Agriculture Organization of the United Nations, accessed January 15, 2021, http://www.fao.org/soils-portal/soil-management/management-of-some-problem-soils/sandy-soils/en/.

9 Joseph Masabni, "Soil Preparation," Texas A&M AgriLife, January 15, 2021, https://agrilifeextension.tamu.edu/library/gardening/soil-preparation/.

10 "Sand, silt or clay? Texture says a lot about soil," Oregon State University, accessed January 15, 2021, https://extension.oregonstate.edu/news/sand-silt-or-clay-texture-says-lot-about-soil.

11 Andrew Dalby, trans., *Geoponika: Farm Work* (Tornes: Prospect Books, 2011), 79.

12 Gilbert L. Wilson, *Native American Gardening: Buffalobird-Woman's Guide to Traditional Methods* (Mineola, NY: Dover Publications, 2005).

13 Environment America Research and Policy Center, "Composting in America," Environment America, June 13, 2019, https://environmentamerica.org/reports/ame/composting-america.

14 Caduto and Bruchac, *Native American Gardening*, 70.

15 Dalby, trans., *Geoponika: Farm Work*, 87.

16 R. K. Prabhu and U.R. Rao, ed., *The Mind of Mahatma Gandhi* (India: Navajivan Mudranalya, 1960), 454.

17 Andrew Dalby, trans., *Geoponika: Farm Work*.

18 Caduto and Bruchac, *Native American Gardening*, 32.

19 Wilson, *Native American Gardening*.

20 Ibid.

21 Ibid.

22

23 Steve Solomon, *Gardening When It Counts: Growing Food in Hard Times* (Gabriola Island, BC: New Society Publishers, 2005)

24 Wilson, *Native American Gardening*.

25 Caduto and Bruchac, *Native American Gardening*, 89.

26 Kathy Weiser-Alexander, "Native American proverbs and Wisdom," Legends of America, updated April 2020, https://www.legendsofamerica.com/na-proverbs/.

27 Grant Gerlock, "Tribes Revive Indigenous Crops, And The Food Traditions That Go With Them," npr, November 18, 2016, https://www.npr.org/sections/thesalt/2016/11/18/502025877/tribes-revive-indigenous-crops-and-the-food-traditions-that-go-with-them.

28 Andi Murphy, "Meet the Three Sisters Who Sustain Native America," PBS: Native Voices, updated November 16, 2018, https://www.pbs.org/native-america/blogs/native-voices/meet-the-three-sisters-who-sustain-native-america/.

29 "Plant Database," Lady Bird Johnson Wildflower Center: The University of Texas at Austin, accessed December 6, 2020, https://www.wildflower.org/plants/result.php?id_plant=HETU.

30 Murphy, "Meet the Three Sisters Who Sustain Native America."

31 "History of Cabbage—Where does Cabbage come from?" Vegetable Facts, accessed December 6, 2020, http://www.vegetablefacts.net/vegetable-history/history-of-cabbage/.

32 "Arugula—Natural Aphrodisiac, Keep the Bedroom Spicy," Underground Health Reporter, April 4, 2013, https://undergroundhealthreporter.com/natural-aphrodisiac.

33 Aisha Gani, "Go back to Halloween's roots and carve a turnip, charity suggests," the Guardian, October 26, 2015, https://www.theguardian.com/lifeandstyle/2015/oct/26/go-back-to-halloweens-roots-and-carve-a-turnip-charity-suggests/.

34 Austine Siomos, "Beets, bacteria and your (micro)biome," Kalispell Regional Healthcare, May 3, 2018, https://www.krh.org/news/beets-bacteria-and-your-microbiome/.

35 Nan Fischer, "The History of Lettuce," Mother Earth Gardener, Spring 2018, https://www.motherearthgardener.com/plant-profiles/edible/the-history-of-lettuce-zm0z18szphe.

36 "Orach: An Ancient Vegetable That's New Again," Laidback Gardener, May 23, 2017, https://laidbackgardener.blog/2017/05/23/orach-an-ancient-vegetable-thats-new-again.

37 "Onion History—Origin and History of Onions," Vegetable Facts, accessed December 6, 2020, http://www.vegetablefacts.net/vegetable-history/history-of-onions/.

38 "Cucumber: A Brief History," Integrated Pest Management: University of Missouri, accessed December 6, 2020, https://ipm.missouri.edu/meg/2014/3/Cucumber-A-Brief-History/.

39 Tim Newman, "All you need to know about beta carotene," MedicalNewsToday, December 14, 2017, https://www.medicalnewstoday.com/articles/25278.

40 "Garden and Landscape Design: Historical Development," Britannica, accessed January 19, 2021, https://www.britannica.com/art/garden-and-landscape-design/ Historical-development.

41 Cameron Lee, "Seminole Pumpkin," Gateway Greening, July 12, 2019, https:// www.gatewaygreening.org/seminole-pumpkin-by-cameron-lee-seung-yul/

42 Ernest Aryeetey et al, eds., *The Oxford Companion to the Economics of Africa* (Oxford, UK: University of Oxford Press, 2012), 266.

43 Ron Krupp, "The Three Sisters," VPR, May 14, 2005, https://archive.vpr.org/ commentary-series/the-three-sisters/.

44 "About the Haudenosaunee Confederacy," Haudenosaunee Confederacy, accessed January 18, 2021, https://www.haudenosauneeconfederacy.com/who-we-are/.

45 J.A. Sandor et al, "Soil Knowledge Embodied in a Native American Runoff Agroecosystem," Iowa State University address, 2002, http://www.uwyo.edu/esm/ faculty-and-staff/jay-norton/papers/wcss02-paper.pdf.

46 "Gifford Delle, "Get To Know Your Polycultures: The Three Sisters," University of Massachusetts at Amherst, July 24, 2013, https://umassdining.com/blog/ sustainability/get-know-your-polycultures-three-sisters .

47 Rich M, "Gardening Wisdom From The Native Americans," Off The Grid News, June 7, 2018, https://www.offthegridnews.com/survival-gardening-2/gardening-wisdom-from-the-native-americans/.

48 Murphy, "Meet the Three Sisters Who Sustain Native America."

49 Ibid.

50 Melissa Miles, "The Art and Science of Making a Hügelkultur Bed – Transforming Woody Debris into a Garden Resource," The Permaculture Research Institute, August 3, 2010, https://www.permaculturenews.org/2010/08/03/the-art-and-science-of-making-a-hugelkultur-bed-transforming-woody-debris-into-a-garden-resource/.

51 Jon R. Stone, *The Routledge Book of World Proverbs* (New York, NY: Routledge, 2006), 94.

52 "Keyhole Gardens Bring Life to Rwandan Village," Garden Media, July 27, 2015, http://www.gardenmediagroup.com/keyhole-gardens-bring-life-rwandan-village.

53 Gilbert L. Wilson, *Buffalo Bird Woman's Garden: Agriculture of the Hidatsa* Indians (St. Paul, MN: Minnesota Historical Society Press, 2006).

54 Clark L. Erickson, "Raised field agriculture in the Lake Titicaca Basin: Putting Ancient Andean Agriculture Back to Work," *Expedition* 30, no. 3 (1988): 8–16, https://www.penn.museum/documents/publications/expedition/PDFs/30-3/Raised. pdf.

55 "Waru Waru, Ancient Andean Irrigation System Brought Back To Life," Ancient Pages, August 8, 2019, http://www.ancientpages.com/2018/04/28/waru-waru-ancient-andean-irrigation-system-brought-back-to-life/.

56 "Chinampas, The Floating Gardens of Mexico."

57 Amorin Mello, "Ancient Garden Beds of Michigan," Chequamegon History, May 5, 2017, https://chequamegonhistory.wordpress.com/2017/05/04/ancient-garden-beds-of-michigan/.

58 Dalby, trans., *Geoponika Farm Work*, 248–9.

59 Paul Fleischman, *Seedfolks* (New York, NY: HarperTrophy, 2004).

60 Barbara Pleasant and Deborah L. Martin, *The Complete Compost Gardening Guide: Banner Batches, Grow Heaps, Comforter Compost, and Other Amazing Techniques for Saving Time and Money, and Producing the Most Flavorful, Nutritious Vegetables Ever* (North Adams, MA: Storey Publishing, 2008).

61 Theophrastus and Arthur Hort, trans., *Enquiry into Plants, Volume I: Books 1–5* (Cambridge, MA: Harvard University Press, 1916), 189.

62 Dalby, *Geoponika: Farm Work*, 89.

63 Wilson, *Native American Gardening*, 116.

64 Dalby, *Geoponika: Farm Work*, 89.

65 Dalby, *Geoponika: Farm Work*, 89, 127.

66 Ibid, 127.

67 Caduto and Bruhac, *Native American Gardening*, 5.

68 Wilson, *Native American Gardening*, 11.

69 Ellen Wulfhorst, "Climate Change is Making Our Food Less Nutritious," World Economic Forum, August 29, 2018, https://www.weforum.org/agenda/2018/08/rising-carbon-levels-threaten-diets-of-hundreds-of-millions-of-poor.

70 John G. Neihardt, *Black Elk Speaks: Being the Life Story of a Holy Man of the Oglala Sioux* (New York, NY: Excelsior Editions, 2008).

71 Dalby, trans., *Geoponika: Farm Work*, 67.

72 Ryrie, *Gardening Folklore that Works*.

73 "What Are the Moon's Phases?" NASA Science Space Place, accessed January 19, 2021, https://spaceplace.nasa.gov/moon-phases/en/.

74 Dalby, trans, *Geoponika: Farm Work*, 59.

75 "How Lunar Planting Works: The Best Lunar Phase and Sign for Increased Vigor," Gardening by the Moon, September 5, 2019, https://www.gardeningbythemoon. com/how-lunar-planting-works/.

76 Oli Holmgren, "Can Moonlight Affect Plant Growth?" Permaculture Principles, August 12, 2018, https://permacultureprinciples.com/post/moonlight-affect-plant-growth/.

77 Caduto and Bruchac, *Native American Gardening*, 16.

78 "Full Moon Names," Old Farmer's Almanac, accessed December 6, 2020, https:// www.almanac.com/content/full-moon-names.

79 Louise Riotte, *Astrological Gardening: The Ancient Wisdom of Successful Planting & Harvesting by the Stars* (North Adams, MA: Storey Publishing, 1995).

80 Arif Mohammed Faisal, "Climate Change and Phenology," *New Age* (2008), http:// blogs.nwic.edu/herbariumblog/files/2011/08/Phenology-and-Climate-Change-UNDP1.pdf.

81 Giovanni Puppi, "Origin and Development of Phenology as a Science," *Italian Journal of Agrometeorology*, no. 3 (2007), http://dwww.agrometeorologia.it/ documenti/Rivista2007_3/pag24.pdf.

82 Wilson, *Native American Gardening*, 22.

83 Jerry Clark, "Greenspace: Phenology Can Offer Garden Planting Guidelines," the *Chippewa Herald*, May 10, 2010, https://chippewa.com/lifestyles/greenspace-phenology-can-offer-garden-planting-guidelines/article_b81b9ef0-5c46-11df-8e96-001cc4c03286.html.

CPSIA information can be obtained
at www.ICGtesting.com
Printed in the USA
LVHW082136170622
721556LV00013B/295